what did JESUS say?

Includes 62 Topics

what did JESUS say?

BIBLE VERSES ON ISSUES YOU DEAL WITH

TYNDALE HOUSE PUBLISHERS, INC.
CAROL STREAM, ILLINOIS

Visit Tyndale's exciting Web site at www.tyndale.com.

TYNDALE and Tyndale's quill logo are registered trademarks of Tyndale House Publishers, Inc.

What Did Jesus Say?: Jesus' Words on 62 Topics

Non-Scripture text by Carolyn Larsen

Cover designed by Beth Sparkman

For manufacturing information regarding this product, please call 1-800-323-9400.

Library of Congress Cataloging-in-Publication Data

Bay, Diane.
   What did Jesus say? : Bible verses on issues you deal with / [created by Diane Bay].
     p. cm.
    ISBN 978-1-4143-3180-5 (sc)
   1. Bible—Indexes. 2. Bible—Quotations. 3. Christian life—Biblical teaching. I. Tyndale House Publishers. II. Title.
    BS432.B34 2010
    248.8'203—dc22   2009046443

Printed in the United States of America

16 15 14 13 12 11 10
7 6 5 4 3 2 1

contents

Abandonment

What a lonely word: abandoned. Left on your own . . . all by yourself . . . alone. Yeah, it's a pretty lonely and scary experience. The feeling of being abandoned can come for different reasons. Sometimes friends turn their backs on you. Sometimes people move away. Sometimes families break up and a dad or mom leaves. Sometimes people die. Any of those things can make you feel abandoned . . . alone. Know what, though? You aren't ever completely alone. Really, you aren't.

Never Alone
Matthew 28:16-20

Then the eleven disciples left for Galilee, going to the mountain where Jesus had told them to go. When they saw him, they worshiped him—but some of them doubted!

Jesus came and told his disciples, "I have been given all authority in heaven and on earth. Therefore, go and make disciples of all the nations, baptizing them in the name of the Father and the Son and the Holy Spirit. Teach these new disciples to obey all the commands I have given you. And be sure of this: I am with you always, even to the end of the age."

Jesus, the Way to the Father
John 14:1-14

"Don't let your hearts be troubled. Trust in God, and trust also in me. There is more than enough room in my Father's home. If this were not so, would I have told you that I am going to prepare a place for you? When everything is ready, I will come and get you, so that you will always be with me where I am. And you know the way to where I am going."

Abandonment

"No, we don't know, Lord," Thomas said. "We have no idea where you are going, so how can we know the way?"

Jesus told him, "I am the way, the truth, and the life. No one can come to the Father except through me. If you had really known me, you would know who my Father is. From now on, you do know him and have seen him!"

Philip said, "Lord, show us the Father, and we will be satisfied."

Jesus replied, "Have I been with you all this time, Philip, and yet you still don't know who I am? Anyone who has seen me has seen the Father! So why are you asking me to show him to you? Don't you believe that I am in the Father and the Father is in me? The words I speak are not my own, but my Father who lives in me does his work through me. Just believe that I am in the Father and the Father is in me. Or at least believe because of the work you have seen me do.

"I tell you the truth, anyone who believes in me will do the same works I have done, and even greater works, because I am going to be with the Father. You can ask for anything in my name, and I will do it, so that the Son can bring glory to the Father. Yes, ask me for anything in my name, and I will do it!"

The Holy Spirit Is Always with You
John 14:15-29

> *Be strong and courageous!*
> *Do not be afraid . . . .*
> *The LORD your God will*
> *personally go ahead of*
> *you. He will neither fail*
> *you nor abandon you.*
>
> —*Deuteronomy 31:6*

"If you love me, obey my commandments. And I will ask the Father, and he will give you another Advocate, who will never leave you. He is the Holy Spirit, who leads into all truth. The world cannot receive him, because it isn't looking for him and doesn't recognize him. But you know him, because he lives with you now and later will be in you. No, I will not abandon you as orphans—I will come to you. Soon the world will no longer see me, but you will see me. Since I live, you also will live. When I am raised to life again, you will know that I am in my Father, and you are in me, and I am in you. Those who accept my commandments and obey them are the ones who love me. And because they love me, my Father will love them. And I will love them and reveal myself to each of them."

Judas (not Judas Iscariot, but the other disciple with that name) said to him, "Lord, why are you going to reveal yourself only to us and not to the world at large?"

Jesus replied, "All who love me will do what I say. My Father will love them, and we will come and make our home with each of them. Anyone who doesn't love me will not obey me. And remember, my words are not my own. What I am telling you is from the Father who sent me. I am telling you these things now while I am still with you. But when the Father sends the Advocate as my representative—that is, the Holy Spirit—he will teach you everything and will remind you of everything I have told you.

"I am leaving you with a gift—peace of mind and heart. And the peace I give is a gift the world cannot give. So don't be troubled or afraid. Remember what I told you: I am going away, but I will come back to you again. If you really loved me, you would be happy that I am going to the Father, who is greater than I am. I have told you these things before they happen so that when they do happen, you will believe."

> *You go before me and follow me. You place your hand of blessing on my head. Such knowledge is too wonderful for me, too great for me to understand! I can never escape from your Spirit! I can never get away from your presence!*
> *—Psalm 139:5-7*

Get it? God is with you. He sent the Holy Spirit to live inside you, so he is always there. You can talk to him whenever you want to. You can tell him whatever is on your mind.

A

No matter what happens with the people in your life, you always have God. Of course, that doesn't mean you don't need people, too. God understands we need someone with skin on, especially when we're feeling sad or lonely, and he can handle that too. He will send someone to be with you—it may not be the person you expected, but he will do it . . . because he loves you. That's the key right there: he loves you. More than you can imagine. So he will stick close to you, listen to you, take care of you, help you, and always love you. You are never alone.

Abilities

What are you a specialist at? Is there something you love to do, something you're really good at? Do you believe you have any special talents? Okay, not that you have some heroic or superhuman abilities or something. But just stop and think about what you like to do, whether it's playing basketball or talking to friends—you do have abilities. And once you know what your abilities are, what will you do with them?

Use Your Abilities Well
Matthew 25:14-30

"The Kingdom of Heaven can be illustrated by the story of a man going on a long trip. He called together his servants and entrusted his money to them while he was gone. He gave five bags of silver to one, two bags of silver to another, and one bag of silver to the last—dividing it in proportion to their abilities. He then left on his trip.

"The servant who received the five bags of silver began to invest the money and earned five more. The servant with two bags of silver also went to work and earned two more. But the servant who received the one bag of silver dug a hole in the ground and hid the master's money.

"After a long time their master returned from his trip and called them to give an account of how they had used his money. The servant to whom he had entrusted the five bags of silver came forward with five more and said, 'Master, you gave me five bags of silver to invest, and I have earned five more.'

"The master was full of praise. 'Well done, my good and faithful servant. You have been faithful in handling this small amount, so now I will give you many more responsibilities. Let's celebrate together!'

> *Dear brothers and sisters, I plead with you to give your bodies to God because of all he has done for you. Let them be a living and holy sacrifice— the kind he will find acceptable. This is truly the way to worship him.*
>
> *—Romans 12:1*

"The servant who had received the two bags of silver came forward and said, 'Master, you gave me two bags of silver to invest, and I have earned two more.'

"The master said, 'Well done, my good and faithful servant. You have been faithful in handling this small amount, so now I will give you many more responsibilities. Let's celebrate together!'

"Then the servant with the one bag of silver came and said, 'Master, I knew you were a harsh man, harvesting crops you didn't plant and gathering crops you didn't cultivate. I was afraid I would lose your money, so I hid it in the earth. Look, here is your money back.'

"But the master replied, 'You wicked and lazy servant! If you knew I harvested crops I didn't plant and gathered crops I didn't cultivate, why didn't you deposit my money in the bank? At least I could have gotten some interest on it.'

Abilities

"Then he ordered, 'Take the money from this servant, and give it to the one with the ten bags of silver. To those who use well what they are given, even more will be given, and they will have an abundance. But from those who do nothing, even what little they have will be taken away. Now throw this useless servant into outer darkness, where there will be weeping and gnashing of teeth.'"

Doing What You're Supposed to Do
Luke 6:43-45

"A good tree can't produce bad fruit, and a bad tree can't produce good fruit. A tree is identified by its fruit. Figs are never gathered from thornbushes, and grapes are not picked from bramble bushes. A good person produces good things from the treasury of a good heart, and an evil person produces evil things from the treasury of an evil heart. What you say flows from what is in your heart."

The bottom line is that God has given you the ability to do something well—maybe more than one something. Doing that thing is one way you can serve him. You don't have to get superspiritual about this—your ability might be something as simple as playing basketball with friends and being fair and including others who don't usually get a chance on the court. It might be showing kindness to someone your classmates don't like much.

Serving God with the abilities he has given you is more important than talking big about what you're going to do for him. Yep, save your breath and just do the stuff he gave you the ability to do. That truly shows your love for him. It also shows that your love for him and your desire to serve him are more than skin deep. If your words about loving God are just words

6

you think you need to say, then they won't be backed up by actions of kindness and love. So . . . they mean nothing. The important thing is to use the abilities God gave you for his work. If you use those talents well, he may give you more abilities and more ways to serve him. That's because he knows you take his work seriously and you'll do your best for him.

> *A spiritual gift is given to each of us so we can help each other.*
> *—1 Corinthians 12:7*

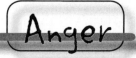

So when's the last time you blew your top? Everyone gets angry sometimes. But did you know God has something to say about that? Yep, he does. God knows you're going to get upset sometimes, but he wants you to respond to your anger in a godly way. He wants you to keep your cool and not say or do things you will be sorry about later.

Anger Is More Than Shouting
Matthew 5:21-22

"You have heard that our ancestors were told, 'You must not murder. If you commit murder, you are subject to judgment.' But I say, if you are even angry with someone, you are subject to judgment! If you call someone an idiot, you are in danger of being brought before the court. And if you curse someone, you are in danger of the fires of hell."

Forgive Already!
Matthew 18:21-35

Peter came to [Jesus] and asked, "Lord, how often should I forgive someone who sins against me? Seven times?"

"No, not seven times," Jesus replied, "but seventy times seven!

"Therefore, the Kingdom of Heaven can be compared to a king who decided to bring his accounts up to date with servants who had borrowed money from him. In the process, one of his debtors was brought in who owed him millions of dollars. He couldn't pay, so his master ordered that he be sold—along with his wife, his children, and everything he owned—to pay the debt.

"But the man fell down before his master and begged him, 'Please, be patient with me, and I will pay it all.' Then his master was filled with pity for him, and he released him and forgave his debt.

"But when the man left the king, he went to a fellow servant who owed him a few thousand dollars. He grabbed him by the throat and demanded instant payment.

"His fellow servant fell down before him and begged for a little more time. 'Be patient with me, and I will pay it,' he pleaded. But his creditor wouldn't wait. He had the man arrested and put in prison until the debt could be paid in full.

> *"Don't sin by letting anger control you."* Don't let the sun go down while you are still angry.
>
> *—Ephesians 4:26*

"When some of the other servants saw this, they were very upset. They went to the king and told him everything that had happened. Then the king called in the man he had forgiven and said, 'You evil servant! I forgave you that tremendous debt because you pleaded with me. Shouldn't you have mercy on your fellow servant, just as I had mercy on you?' Then the angry king sent the man to prison to be tortured until he had paid his entire debt.

"That's what my heavenly Father will do to you if you refuse to forgive your brothers and sisters from your heart."

The Story of the Lost Son
Luke 15:11-32

Jesus told them this story: "A man had two sons. The younger son told his father, 'I want my share of your estate now before you die.' So his father agreed to divide his wealth between his sons.

"A few days later this younger son packed all his belongings and moved to a distant land, and there he wasted all his money in wild living. About the time his money ran out, a great famine swept over the land, and he began to starve. He persuaded a local farmer to hire him, and the man sent him into his fields to feed the pigs. The young man became so hungry that even the pods he was feeding the pigs looked good to him. But no one gave him anything.

"When he finally came to his senses, he said to himself, 'At home even the hired servants have food enough to spare, and here I am dying of hunger! I will go home to my father and say, "Father, I have sinned against both heaven and you, and I am no longer worthy of being called your son. Please take me on as a hired servant."'

"So he returned home to his father. And while he was still a long way off, his father saw him coming. Filled with love and compassion, he ran to his son, embraced him, and kissed him. His son said to him, 'Father, I have sinned against both heaven and you, and I am no longer worthy of being called your son.'

"But his father said to the servants, 'Quick! Bring the finest robe in the house and put it on him. Get a ring for his finger and sandals for his feet. And kill the calf we have been fattening. We must celebrate with a feast, for this son of mine was dead and has now returned to life. He was lost, but now he is found.' So the party began.

"Meanwhile, the older son was in the fields working. When he returned home, he heard music and dancing in the house, and he asked one of the servants what was going on. 'Your brother is back,' he was told, 'and your father has killed

B

the fattened calf. We are celebrating because of his safe return.'

"The older brother was angry and wouldn't go in. His father came out and begged him, but he replied, 'All these years I've slaved for you and never once refused to do a single thing you told me to. And in all that time you never gave me even one young goat for a feast with my friends.

> *Human anger does not produce the righteousness God desires.*
>
> *—James 1:20*

Yet when this son of yours comes back after squandering your money on prostitutes, you celebrate by killing the fattened calf!'

"His father said to him, 'Look, dear son, you have always stayed by me, and everything I have is yours. We had to celebrate this happy day. For your brother was dead and has come back to life! He was lost, but now he is found!'"

> *People may be right in their own eyes, but the LORD examines their heart.*
>
> *—Proverbs 21:2*

Anger can make people do ugly things: yell, fight, cheat, or hold a long, hard grudge. People get angry—that's a fact. But how you handle anger is the key. When you are hurt or angry, there is a temptation to say mean things or refuse to forgive, even if the person apologizes for his or her actions. When you are angry, remember what Jesus said the most important commandments are: to love God and to love others. Love and anger can't fill the same space in your heart, so don't let anger take the place of love.

Belief

You probably know in your mind what you truly believe—you know, about God and living for him. But here's the question: do you believe it enough to live it? When your friends are spouting this or

that about what they think is right or acceptable in life, do you just go along with them? Or do your beliefs mean enough to you that you'll stand up for them, even if someone gives you a hard time about them?

Belief That Stands Strong
Matthew 7:24-27

"Anyone who listens to my teaching and follows it is wise, like a person who builds a house on solid rock. Though the rain comes in torrents and the floodwaters rise and the winds beat against that house, it won't collapse because it is built on bedrock. But anyone who hears my teaching and doesn't obey it is foolish, like a person who builds a house on sand. When the rains and floods come and the winds beat against that house, it will collapse with a mighty crash."

Belief That Gives All
Matthew 16:24-27

Jesus said to his disciples, "If any of you wants to be my follower, you must turn from your selfish ways, take up your cross, and follow me. If you try to hang on to your life, you will lose it. But if you give up your life for my sake, you will save it. And what do you benefit if you gain the whole world but lose your own soul? Is anything worth more than your soul? For the Son of Man will come with his angels in the glory of his Father and will judge all people according to their deeds. And I tell you the truth, some standing here right now will not die before they see the Son of Man coming in his Kingdom."

Belief That Takes Root
Luke 8:4-15

One day Jesus told a story in the form of a parable to a large crowd that had gathered from many towns to hear him: "A farmer went out to plant his seed. As he scattered it across his field, some seed fell on a foot-path, where it was stepped on, and the

B

birds ate it. Other seed fell among rocks. It began to grow, but the plant soon wilted and died for lack of moisture. Other seed fell among thorns that grew up with it and choked out the tender plants. Still other seed fell on fertile soil. This seed grew and produced a crop that was a hundred times as much as had been planted!" When he had said this, he called out, "Anyone with ears to hear should listen and understand."

His disciples asked him what this parable meant. He replied, "You are permitted to understand the secrets of the Kingdom of God. But I use parables to teach the others so that the Scriptures might be fulfilled:

'When they look, they won't really see.
When they hear, they won't understand.'

"This is the meaning of the parable: The seed is God's word. The seeds that fell on the footpath represent those who hear the message, only to have the devil come and take it away from their hearts and prevent them from believing and being saved. The seeds on the rocky soil represent those who hear the message and receive it with joy. But since they don't have deep roots, they believe for a while, then they fall away when they face temptation. The seeds that fell among the thorns represent those who hear the message, but all too quickly the message is crowded out by the cares and riches

> *You must continue to believe this truth and stand firmly in it.*
>
> *—Colossians 1:23*

and pleasures of this life. And so they never grow into maturity. And the seeds that fell on the good soil represent honest, good-hearted people who hear God's word, cling to it, and patiently produce a huge harvest."

You can say you believe just about anything, and then you can change what you say depending on which friends you're with. Then you can do whatever those friends are doing just so you can fit in with them. But that's not how it should be. You see, believing in God and his Word leads to trusting him, which leads to obeying him, which leads to living your life in a way that pleases him. You might be able to put on a good show and fool people around you about what you believe, but you can't fool God. He doesn't accept an on-again, off-again obedience. In fact, there is a verse in the book of Revelation where he says he will spit "lukewarm" believers out of his mouth (Revelation 3:16). Whoa! You don't want to be in that category!

So if you believe that Jesus died for your sins and rose from the dead, if you believe that God's Word is his story and that every word in it speaks of how powerful, amazing, loving, and wise he is—if you really *believe all that*—it will show in your life! How? By the way you keep his commandments, by the kindness and love you show to others, by your honesty and fairness, by your concern for others, by the way you tell others that God loves them, by your willingness to think of others before yourself . . . the list goes on.

If you think that takes a lot of effort—you're right! But it's not stuff you have to do on your own. Because if you believe in God and if you've asked Jesus into your life, he will help you. The bottom line is that no matter how hard you try to put up a good front, your true beliefs will always seep through into your life—what you believe will show in how you live. So decide what you believe, and live like you mean it!

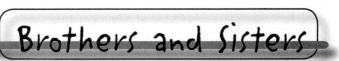

Brothers and Sisters

Brothers can be a pain in the neck . . . and so can sisters, for that matter. Getting along with the people you live with is not always easy. Why is that? Maybe it's because you are so comfortable with family

Brothers and Sisters

B

members that you don't make the effort to be nice and respectful toward them. But did you know that Jesus cares about the way you treat your brothers and sisters? And it's not just your actual family he's concerned about. He also cares about the brothers and sisters you have from being a part of God's family.

How You Treat Others Matters

Matthew 18:1-10

The disciples came to Jesus and asked, "Who is greatest in the Kingdom of Heaven?"

Jesus called a little child to him and put the child among them. Then he said, "I tell you the truth, unless you turn from your sins and become like little children, you will never get into the Kingdom of Heaven. So anyone who becomes as humble as this little child is the greatest in the Kingdom of Heaven.

"And anyone who welcomes a little child like this on my behalf is welcoming me. But if you cause one of these little ones who trusts in me to fall into sin, it would be better for you to have a large millstone tied around your neck and be drowned in the depths of the sea.

"What sorrow awaits the world, because it tempts people to sin. Temptations are inevitable, but what sorrow awaits the person who does the tempting. So if your hand or foot causes you to sin, cut it off and throw it away. It's better to enter eternal life with only one hand or one foot than to be thrown into eternal fire with both of your hands and feet. And if your eye causes you to sin, gouge it out and throw it away. It's better to enter eternal life with only one eye than to have two eyes and be thrown into the fire of hell.

"Beware that you don't look down on any of these little ones. For I tell you that in heaven their angels are always in the presence of my heavenly Father."

Keeping the Peace
Matthew 18:15-20

"If another believer sins against you, go privately and point out the offense. If the other person listens and confesses it, you have won that person back.

> *Respect everyone, and love your Christian brothers and sisters.*
>
> *—1 Peter 2:17*

But if you are unsuccessful, take one or two others with you and go back again, so that everything you say may be confirmed by two or three witnesses. If the person still refuses to listen, take your case to the church. Then if he or she won't accept the church's decision, treat that person as a pagan or a corrupt tax collector.

"I tell you the truth, whatever you forbid on earth will be forbidden in heaven, and whatever you permit on earth will be permitted in heaven.

"I also tell you this: If two of you agree here on earth concerning anything you ask, my Father in heaven will do it for you. For where two or three gather together as my followers, I am there among them."

The Greatest Love
John 15:1-17

"I am the true grapevine, and my Father is the gardener. He cuts off every branch of mine that doesn't produce fruit, and he prunes the branches that do bear fruit so they will produce even more. You have already been pruned and purified by the message I have given you. Remain in me, and I will remain in you. For a branch cannot produce fruit if it is severed from the vine, and you cannot be fruitful unless you remain in me.

"Yes, I am the vine; you are the branches. Those who remain in me, and I in them, will produce much fruit. For apart from me you can do nothing. Anyone who does not remain in me is thrown away like a useless branch and withers. Such branches are gathered into a pile to be burned. But if you remain in me and my words remain in you, you may ask for anything you want, and it will be granted! When you produce much fruit, you are my true disciples. This brings great glory to my Father.

Brothers and Sisters

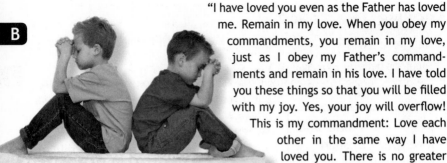

B

"I have loved you even as the Father has loved me. Remain in my love. When you obey my commandments, you remain in my love, just as I obey my Father's commandments and remain in his love. I have told you these things so that you will be filled with my joy. Yes, your joy will overflow! This is my commandment: Love each other in the same way I have loved you. There is no greater love than to lay down one's life for one's friends. You are my friends if you do what I command. I no longer call you slaves, because a master doesn't confide in his slaves. Now you are my friends, since I have told you everything the Father told me. You didn't choose me. I chose you. I appointed you to go and produce lasting fruit, so that the Father will give you whatever you ask for, using my name. This is my command: Love each other."

Jesus' Family

Mark 3:31-35

Jesus' mother and brothers came to see him. They stood outside and sent word for him to come out and talk with them. There was a crowd sitting around Jesus, and someone said, "Your mother and your brothers are outside asking for you."

Jesus replied, "Who is my mother? Who are my brothers?" Then he looked at those around him and said, "Look, these are my mother and brothers. Anyone who does God's will is my brother and sister and mother."

The family you were born into is not the only family you have. Sure you may have a mom, dad, brothers, sisters, or other relatives. And when you hear about brothers and sisters, you probably think of the family you live with, and either you're filled with warm, fuzzy feelings for them or (if you're having a bad day) you may think about what a pain they are and how it's not fair that God asks you to get along with them and love them. But did you know that it matters to God whether or not you get along with his family too? Whatever causes you to have trouble getting along with others, take care of it. The strength and help you need to keep your relationships strong come from staying close to God—reading his Word and asking him for help.

Compassion

C

Nobody wants to be around a person who has no compassion. People like that have no heart and no desire to be kind or helpful to others. They don't care when people around them are in pain or grieving. They seem to be made of stone. Without compassion, we can't feel for other people— either joy or sorrow. The way Jesus lived modeled care and compassion to the people he interacted with. He felt the pain of the people around him who were sad or hurting, and he did something about it.

Caring for People in Need
Matthew 9:9-13

As Jesus was walking along, he saw a man named Matthew sitting at his tax collector's booth. "Follow me and be my disciple," Jesus said to him. So Matthew got up and followed him.

Later, Matthew invited Jesus and his disciples to his home as dinner guests, along with many tax collectors and other disreputable sinners. But when the Pharisees saw this, they asked his disciples, "Why does your teacher eat with such scum?"

When Jesus heard this, he said, "Healthy people don't need a doctor—sick people do." Then he added, "Now go and learn the meaning of this Scripture: 'I want you to show mercy, not offer sacrifices.' For I have come to call not those who think they are righteous, but those who know they are sinners."

Jesus' Compassion
Matthew 11:25-30

C

Jesus prayed this prayer: "O Father, Lord of heaven and earth, thank you for hiding these things from those who think themselves wise and clever, and for revealing them to the childlike. Yes, Father, it pleased you to do it this way!

> *The faithful love of the LORD never ends! His mercies never cease.*
>
> *—Lamentations 3:22*

"My Father has entrusted everything to me. No one truly knows the Son except the Father, and no one truly knows the Father except the Son and those to whom the Son chooses to reveal him."

Then Jesus said, "Come to me, all of you who are weary and carry heavy burdens, and I will give you rest. Take my yoke upon you. Let me teach you, because I am humble and gentle at heart, and you will find rest for your souls. For my yoke is easy to bear, and the burden I give you is light."

Jesus Cares for the Lost
Matthew 18:12-14

"If a man has a hundred sheep and one of them wanders away, what will he do? Won't he leave the ninety-nine others on the hills and go out to search for the one that is lost? And if he finds it, I tell you the truth, he will rejoice over it more than over the ninety-nine that didn't wander away! In the same way, it is not my heavenly Father's will that even one of these little ones should perish."

Jesus Wants to Help
Luke 5:12-15

In one of the villages, Jesus met a man with an advanced case of leprosy. When the man saw Jesus, he bowed with his face to the ground, begging to be healed. "Lord," he said, "if you are willing, you can heal me and make me clean."

Jesus reached out and touched him. "I am willing," he said. "Be healed!" And instantly the leprosy disappeared. Then Jesus instructed him not to tell anyone what had happened. He said, "Go to the priest and let him examine you. Take along the offering required in the law of Moses for those who have been healed of leprosy. This will be a public testimony that you have been cleansed."

C

But despite Jesus' instructions, the report of his power spread even faster, and vast crowds came to hear him preach and to be healed of their diseases.

The thing about compassion is that it is not just caring about others and the things they are going through. Real compassion puts that caring into action. When you read about Jesus meeting someone who was sick or hurting, he didn't just say, "Oh, that's too bad. I feel sorry for you." He did something about it. Now, can you heal the sick or raise the dead? Not so much. But there is always something you can do. Sometimes it's giving your time and energy to physically help someone. That could mean raking leaves for an older neighbor. It could mean being there for a friend who is going through a tough time. It might mean helping out more around the house when your mom and dad are busy. Sometimes compassion involves giving money to missionaries or organizations that help people in your own city and around the world who are struggling to make it day by day.

And there is one more powerful, effective way that you can put your compassion into action: pray! Granted, sometimes that feels inactive, but it really isn't. Pray for God to act in a person's life. Pray for the person's

> *Be kind to each other, tenderhearted, forgiving one another, just as God through Christ has forgiven you.*
> *—Ephesians 4:32*

Courage

attention to be turned to God and focused on his love and care. Pray for God's glory to be shown in the situation. Pray. Pray. Pray. Pray with a compassionate, trusting heart, and be ready for what God will do!

Have you ever bragged about how brave you are? Yeah, you're not scared of anything, right? But here's a secret about courage: it's not exactly the opposite of fear. Courage isn't foolish bragging that melts away when things get really scary. Courage isn't just about doing what you might be afraid of—it's also about having the strength to take a stand even if no one else will.

Courage in Hard Times
Matthew 16:21-28

Jesus began to tell his disciples plainly that it was necessary for him to go to Jerusalem, and that he would suffer many terrible things at the hands of the elders, the leading priests, and the teachers of religious law. He would be killed, but on the third day he would be raised from the dead.

But Peter took him aside and began to reprimand him for saying such things. "Heaven forbid, Lord," he said. "This will never happen to you!"

Jesus turned to Peter and said, "Get away from me, Satan! You are a dangerous trap to me. You are seeing things merely from a human point of view, not from God's."

Then Jesus said to his disciples, "If any of you wants to be my follower, you must turn from your selfish ways, take up your cross, and follow me. If you try to hang on to your life, you will lose it. But if you give up your life for my sake, you will save it. And what do you benefit if you gain the whole world but lose your own soul? Is anything worth more than your soul? For the Son of Man will come with his angels in the glory of his Father and will judge all people according to their deeds. And I tell you the truth, some standing here right now will not die before they see the Son of Man coming in his Kingdom."

Stand Strong
Luke 12:1-12

The crowds grew until thousands were milling about and stepping on each other. Jesus turned first to his disciples and warned them, "Beware

> *This is my command—be strong and courageous! Do not be afraid or discouraged. For the LORD your God is with you wherever you go.*
>
> *—Joshua 1:9*

of the yeast of the Pharisees—their hypocrisy. The time is coming when everything that is covered up will be revealed, and all that is secret will be made known to all. Whatever you have said in the dark will be heard in the light, and what you have whispered behind closed doors will be shouted from the housetops for all to hear!

"Dear friends, don't be afraid of those who want to kill your body; they cannot do any more to you after that. But I'll tell you whom to fear. Fear God, who has the power to kill you and then throw you into hell. Yes, he's the one to fear.

"What is the price of five sparrows—two copper coins? Yet God does not forget a single one of them. And the very hairs on your head are all numbered. So don't be afraid; you are more valuable to God than a whole flock of sparrows.

"I tell you the truth, everyone who acknowledges me publicly here on earth, the Son of Man will also acknowledge in the presence of God's angels. But anyone who denies me here on earth will be denied before God's angels. Anyone who speaks against the Son of Man can be forgiven, but anyone who blasphemes the Holy Spirit will not be forgiven.

"And when you are brought to trial in the synagogues and before rulers and authorities, don't worry about how to defend yourself or what to say, for the

Holy Spirit will teach you at that time what needs to be said."

Courage from Prayer

C

Luke 22:39-44

> *I can do everything through Christ, who gives me strength.*
> *—Philippians 4:13*

Accompanied by the disciples, Jesus left the upstairs room and went as usual to the Mount of Olives. There he told them, "Pray that you will not give in to temptation."

He walked away, about a stone's throw, and knelt down and prayed, "Father, if you are willing, please take this cup of suffering away from me. Yet I want your will to be done, not mine." Then an angel from heaven appeared and strengthened him. He prayed more fervently, and he was in such agony of spirit that his sweat fell to the ground like great drops of blood.

Can you do the right thing when everyone else is doing the wrong thing? When a bunch of your friends are doing something you know is wrong, do you have the courage to say, "No, thanks. Not for me"? When the people you hang out with start picking on someone because he's kind of a geek or just so easy to make fun of, do you have the courage to not join in? If your best friends start checking out some Web sites you know you shouldn't be looking at, are you courageous enough to walk away? Courage isn't always easy, because it isn't always popular.

Courage isn't so much about not being afraid—it involves the wisdom to know the difference between right and wrong and then acting on that wisdom—doing what is right, even if you're standing alone. No one likes to be considered weird. But even if you feel alone, you really aren't. The Holy Spirit lives in you. He will give you the wisdom to make the right decisions. And he will give you the courage to follow through on them. Jesus courageously faced his own death, and his strength will help you face whatever life brings your way. Have the courage to take a stand for him, and he will be there for you . . . always!

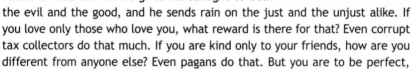

Enemies

Maybe you've never been in a literal war, but chances are you've still had an enemy or two. But what makes a person become an enemy in the first place? It's usually because the person hurt you—physically or emotionally—or hurt your reputation. Then you want to hurt him or her back and get even. Before you know it, you've got an enemy. But what does God's Word say about how you should treat your enemies?

Loving Those Who Are Hard to Love

Matthew 5:43-48

"You have heard the law that says, 'Love your neighbor' and hate your enemy. But I say, love your enemies! Pray for those who persecute you! In that way, you will be acting as true children of your Father in heaven. For he gives his sunlight to both the evil and the good, and he sends rain on the just and the unjust alike. If you love only those who love you, what reward is there for that? Even corrupt tax collectors do that much. If you are kind only to your friends, how are you different from anyone else? Even pagans do that. But you are to be perfect, even as your Father in heaven is perfect."

> *Hatred stirs up quarrels, but love makes up for all offenses.*
>
> *—Proverbs 10:12*

Loving God Most

Matthew 5:21-24

"You have heard that our ancestors were told, 'You must not murder. If you commit murder, you are subject to judgment.' But I say, if you are even angry with someone, you are subject to judgment! If you call someone an idiot, you are in danger of being brought before the court. And if you curse someone, you are in danger of the fires of hell.

"So if you are presenting a sacrifice at the altar in the Temple and you suddenly remember that someone has something against you, leave your sacrifice there at the altar. Go and be reconciled to that person. Then come and offer your sacrifice to God."

How to Treat Your Enemies

Luke 6:37-42

"Do not judge others, and you will not be judged. Do not condemn others, or it will all come back against you. Forgive others, and you will be forgiven. Give, and you will receive. Your gift will return to you in full—pressed down, shaken together to make room for more, running over, and poured into your lap. The amount you give will determine the amount you get back."

Then Jesus gave the following illustration: "Can one blind person lead another? Won't they both fall into a ditch? Students are not greater than their teacher. But the student who is fully trained will become like the teacher.

May the Lord make your love for one another and for all people grow and overflow, just as our love for you overflows.

—1 Thessalonians 3:12

"And why worry about a speck in your friend's eye when you have a log in your own? How can you think of saying, 'Friend, let me help you get rid of that speck in your eye,' when you can't see past the log in your own eye? Hypocrite! First get rid of the log in your own eye; then you will see well enough to deal with the speck in your friend's eye."

So you love your friends . . . big deal. Anyone can do that. Even the meanest dude you can think of has friends he cares about and sticks up for. It doesn't take any superpowers to love your friends. What is tough is loving your enemies. Not just saying you love them, but actually meaning it. Let's be honest—it's hard to love people who aren't very lovable. It's hard to want good things for people who are mean to you. In fact, it's so hard that you simply can't do it—at least, not by yourself. But God's love working through you can make it happen. If you're going to follow God's model, then you absolutely have to love your enemies. There are a couple of steps to this.

First, stop letting yourself off the hook. Don't criticize someone else's behavior when yours is not perfect (and never will be).

Second, cut other people a little slack. Remember, they may be fighting their own battles of self-esteem or criticism or problems at home.

Third, remember how much and how often God forgives you. If he can forgive you so often and so much, it should give you the perspective to forgive others.

This life is a journey, and we're all on it together . . . so don't think only about yourself and how everything affects you. Think about others. Pray for them. Forgive them. Love them (okay, let God love them through you). Pretty soon you'll find your list of enemies shrinking fast.

When God created the world and the first people, everything he made was good. His plan was for people to live according to his standards—to be obedient to him and love him. But God gave people the freedom to choose between good and evil, and sometimes they choose evil.

Evil on the Inside
Matthew 15:1-20

Some Pharisees and teachers of religious law now arrived from Jerusalem to see Jesus. They asked him, "Why do your disciples disobey our age-old tradition? For they ignore our tradition of ceremonial hand washing before they eat."

Jesus replied, "And why do you, by your traditions, violate the direct commandments of God? For instance, God says, 'Honor your father and mother,' and 'Anyone who speaks disrespectfully of father or mother must be put to death.' But you say it is all right for people to say to their parents, 'Sorry, I can't help you. For I have vowed to give to God what I would have given to you.' In this way, you say they don't need to honor their parents. And so you cancel the word of God for the sake of your own tradition. You hypocrites! Isaiah was right when he prophesied about you, for he wrote,

'These people honor me with their lips,
but their hearts are far from me.
Their worship is a farce,
for they teach man-made ideas as commands from God.'"

Then Jesus called to the crowd to come and hear. "Listen," he said, "and try to understand. It's not what goes into your mouth that defiles you; you are defiled by the words that come out of your mouth."

Then the disciples came to him and asked, "Do you realize you offended the Pharisees by what you just said?"

Jesus replied, "Every plant not planted by my heavenly Father will be uprooted, so ignore them. They are blind guides leading the blind, and if one blind person guides another, they will both fall into a ditch."

Then Peter said to Jesus, "Explain to us the parable that says people aren't defiled by what they eat."

"Don't you understand yet?" Jesus asked. "Anything you eat passes through the stomach and then goes into the sewer. But the words you speak come from the heart—that's what defiles you. For from the heart come evil thoughts, murder, adultery, all sexual immorality, theft, lying, and slander. These are what defile you. Eating with unwashed hands will never defile you."

Evil Actions
Mark 12:1-11

Jesus began teaching them with stories: "A man planted a vineyard. He built a wall around it, dug a pit for pressing out the grape juice, and built a lookout tower. Then he leased the vineyard to tenant farmers and moved to another country. At the time of the grape harvest, he sent one of his servants to collect his share of the crop. But the farmers grabbed the servant, beat him up, and sent him back empty-handed. The owner then sent another servant, but they insulted him and beat him over the head. The next servant he sent was killed.

Evil

Others he sent were either beaten or killed, until there was only one left—his son whom he loved dearly. The owner finally sent him, thinking, 'Surely they will respect my son.'

"But the tenant farmers said to one another, 'Here comes the heir to this estate. Let's kill him and get the estate for ourselves!' So they grabbed him and murdered him and threw his body out of the vineyard.

E

"What do you suppose the owner of the vineyard will do?" Jesus asked. "I'll tell you—he will come and kill those farmers and lease the vineyard to others. Didn't you ever read this in the Scriptures?

> 'The stone that the builders rejected has now become the cornerstone.
> This is the LORD's doing, and it is wonderful to see.'"

> *His unfailing love toward those who fear him is as great as the height of the heavens above the earth. He has removed our sins as far from us as the east is from the west.*
>
> *—Psalm 103:11-12*

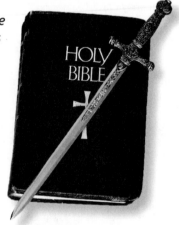

Jesus warned his followers that they have to battle evil in the world in their efforts to live for him. Evil is all around. Satan—God's archenemy—does everything he can to pull God's followers away from obeying God. But when the Holy Spirit fills you with his power, you have the strength to fight off the evil that tries to control you. You see, if the Holy Spirit lives in you and you are trying to obey God, then you know the way you should live. However, if you aren't obeying God, then evil is controlling you.

Evil is a powerful force in this world. Don't ignore it . . . and don't let it control you. There is a way to fight it off—ask Jesus to be the one in control of your life. Push evil away, and don't let it get a grip on your heart! Jesus promises that he will help you fight it off. Whatever is in your heart eventually shows up in your life—whether it's evil or good.

What comes to mind when you think about faith? Maybe it seems like kind of a churchy word, but another way to think of it is trust, confidence, belief, or devotion. The real question is, what or who do you put your faith in? What would you be willing to entrust your health, safety, or even your life to?

F

Courageous faith

Matthew 8:5-13

> *Faith is the confidence that what we hope for will actually happen; it gives us assurance about things we cannot see.*
>
> *—Hebrews 11:1*

When Jesus returned to Capernaum, a Roman officer came and pleaded with him, "Lord, my young servant lies in bed, paralyzed and in terrible pain."

Jesus said, "I will come and heal him."

But the officer said, "Lord, I am not worthy to have you come into my home. Just say the word from where you are, and my servant will be healed. I know this because I am under the authority of my superior officers, and I have authority over my soldiers. I only need to say, 'Go,' and they go, or 'Come,' and they come. And if I say to my slaves, 'Do this,' they do it."

When Jesus heard this, he was amazed. Turning to those who were following him, he said, "I tell you the truth, I haven't seen faith like this in all Israel! And I tell you this, that many Gentiles will come from all over the world—from east and west—and sit down with Abraham, Isaac, and Jacob at the feast in the Kingdom of Heaven. But many Israelites—those for whom the Kingdom was prepared—will be thrown into outer darkness, where there will be weeping and gnashing of teeth."

Then Jesus said to the Roman officer, "Go back home. Because you believed, it has happened." And the young servant was healed that same hour.

F

See and Believe
Mark 4:35-41

As evening came, Jesus said to his disciples, "Let's cross to the other side of the lake." So they took Jesus in the boat and started out, leaving the crowds behind (although other boats followed). But soon a fierce storm came up. High waves were breaking into the boat, and it began to fill with water.

Jesus was sleeping at the back of the boat with his head on a cushion. The disciples woke him up, shouting, "Teacher, don't you care that we're going to drown?"

When Jesus woke up, he rebuked the wind and said to the waves, "Silence! Be still!" Suddenly the wind stopped, and there was a great calm. Then he asked them, "Why are you afraid? Do you still have no faith?"

The disciples were absolutely terrified. "Who is this man?" they asked each other. "Even the wind and waves obey him!"

Faith in Action
Mark 11:12-14, 20-25

As they were leaving Bethany, Jesus was hungry. He noticed a fig tree in full leaf a little way off, so he went over to see if he could find any figs. But there were only leaves because it was too early in the season for fruit. Then Jesus said to the tree, "May no one ever eat your fruit again!" And the disciples heard him say it. . . .

The next morning as they passed by the fig tree he had cursed, the disciples noticed it had withered from the roots up. Peter remembered what Jesus had said to the

> *Dear brothers and sisters, when troubles come your way, consider it an opportunity for great joy. For you know that when your faith is tested, your endurance has a chance to grow. So let it grow, for when your endurance is fully developed, you will be perfect and complete, needing nothing.*
>
> *—James 1:2-4*

tree on the previous day and exclaimed, "Look, Rabbi! The fig tree you cursed has withered and died!"

Then Jesus said to the disciples, "Have faith in God. I tell you the truth, you can say to this mountain, 'May you be lifted up and thrown into the sea,' and it will happen. But you must really believe it will happen and have no doubt in your heart. I tell you, you can pray for anything, and if you believe that you've received it, it will be yours. But when you are praying, first forgive anyone you are holding a grudge against, so that your Father in heaven will forgive your sins, too."

> *This Good News tells us how God makes us right in his sight. This is accomplished from start to finish by faith. As the Scriptures say, "It is through faith that a righteous person has life."*
> *—Romans 1:17*

F

Is faith something you can conjure up? Can you just make yourself believe in something or someone? No. There has to be some kind of relationship to begin the faith process—you respect someone, you see things in that person that make you trust him or her, you believe that person cares about you. It's one thing to know the right answers and talk about your faith in God. But do you really, really believe?

Faith in God is more than just believing in him. It's more than just head knowledge. Faith means you trust him enough to obey his commands and let him guide your life. Look at these stories from Scripture—a high-level army officer risks having his fellow soldiers make fun of him to show his faith in Jesus. In the other two stories, Jesus tells his followers that having a real, honest faith in him gives great power . . . his power. How cool is that? This kind of faith is willing to take a powerful, strong stand for Jesus. This kind of faith lets the world know you believe in him no matter what—no matter what your friends think, no matter how hard life gets. You trust him completely. That's true faith.

Maybe you don't like to admit it when you're scared of something . . . or maybe everyone knows you're scared of a ton of things. Fear does weird things to a person. When you have that knot of fear in the pit of your stomach, you find out what you really believe, who you really trust. Where do you turn to find safety? Do you turn to friends or to addictions and physical comforts, or do you go to the only One who can truly offer safety?

Jesus' Friends Are Scared
Luke 8:22-25

One day Jesus said to his disciples, "Let's cross to the other side of the lake." So they got into a boat and started out. As they sailed across, Jesus settled down for a nap. But soon a fierce storm came down on the lake. The boat was filling with water, and they were in real danger.

The disciples went and woke him up, shouting, "Master, Master, we're going to drown!"

When Jesus woke up, he rebuked the wind and the raging waves. Suddenly the storm stopped and all was calm. Then he asked them, "Where is your faith?"

The disciples were terrified and amazed. "Who is this man?" they asked each other. "When he gives a command, even the wind and waves obey him!"

How to Face Your Fears
Luke 4:1-12

Jesus, full of the Holy Spirit, returned from the Jordan River. He was led by the Spirit in the wilderness, where he was tempted by the devil for forty days. Jesus ate nothing all that time and became very hungry.

Then the devil said to him, "If you are the Son of God, tell this stone to become a loaf of bread."

But Jesus told him, "No! The Scriptures say, 'People do not live by bread alone.'"

Then the devil took him up and revealed to him all the kingdoms of the world in a moment of time. "I will give you the glory of these kingdoms and authority over them," the devil said, "because they are mine to give to anyone I please. I will give it all to you if you will worship me."

Jesus replied, "The Scriptures say, 'You must worship the LORD your God and serve only him.'"

Then the devil took him to Jerusalem, to the highest point of the Temple, and said, "If you are the Son of God, jump off! For the Scriptures say, 'He will order his angels to protect and guard you. And they will hold you up with their hands so you won't even hurt your foot on a stone.'"

Jesus responded, "The Scriptures also say, 'You must not test the LORD your God.'"

> *God is our refuge and strength, always ready to help in times of trouble. So we will not fear when earthquakes come and the mountains crumble into the sea.*
>
> *—Psalm 46:1-2*

Where Courage Comes From
John 14:1-7

"Don't let your hearts be troubled. Trust in God, and trust also in me. There is more than enough room in my Father's home. If this were not so, would I have told you that I am going to prepare a place for you? When everything is ready,

F

I will come and get you, so that you will always be with me where I am. And you know the way to where I am going."

"No, we don't know, Lord," Thomas said. "We have no idea where you are going, so how can we know the way?"

Jesus told him, "I am the way, the truth, and the life. No one can come to the Father except through me. If you had really known me, you would know who my Father is. From now on, you do know him and have seen him!"

Jesus Promises Help
Luke 24:35-49

The two from Emmaus told their story of how Jesus had appeared to them as they were walking along the road, and how they had recognized him as he was breaking the bread. And just as they were telling about it, Jesus himself was suddenly standing there among them. "Peace be with you," he said. But the whole group was startled and frightened, thinking they were seeing a ghost!

"Why are you frightened?" he asked. "Why are your hearts filled with doubt? Look at my hands. Look at my feet. You can see that it's really me. Touch me and make sure that I am not a ghost, because ghosts don't have bodies, as you see that I do." As he spoke, he showed them his hands and his feet.

Still they stood there in disbelief, filled with joy and wonder. Then he asked them, "Do you have anything here to eat?" They gave him a piece of broiled fish, and he ate it as they watched.

Then he said, "When I was with you before, I told you that everything written about me in the law of Moses and the prophets and in the Psalms must be fulfilled." Then he opened their minds to understand the Scriptures. And he said, "Yes, it was written long ago that the Messiah would suffer and die and rise from the dead on the third day. It was also written that this message would be proclaimed in the authority of his name to all the nations, beginning in Jerusalem: 'There is forgiveness of sins for all who repent.' You are witnesses of all these things.

"And now I will send the Holy Spirit, just as my Father promised. But stay here in the city until the Holy Spirit comes and fills you with power from heaven."

No doubt about it, sometimes life is scary—people do awful things to each other, and there's a lot of evil in the world. Yeah, it's scary. It's not always a bad thing to be scared—in fact, sometimes that protects you and makes you more cautious. But you don't have to be a slave to fear when you know that your protection comes from God. That's why it's important to read his Word and get to know him. He is more powerful than anything and smarter than everyone, and he loves you very, very much. Go to him when you're scared. He's there for you!

> *Don't be afraid, for I am with you. Don't be discouraged, for I am your God.*
> *—Isaiah 41:10*

F

forgiveness

When we do something wrong, we're quick to think our friends should forgive us. We assume they should know what we "meant to say" or that we acted that way because we were just having a bad day.

We also think that God should cut us some slack for the ways we mess up . . . and forgive us. But here's an interesting question to think about: Do we offer that same grace to others? How quick are we to forgive when we're on the other side of things?

Do You Have to Forgive Everyone?

Matthew 5:43-48

"You have heard the law that says, 'Love your neighbor' and hate your enemy. But I say, love your enemies! Pray for those who persecute you! In that way, you will be acting as true children of your Father in heaven. For he gives his sunlight to both the evil and the good, and he sends rain on the just and the unjust alike. If you love only those who love you, what reward is there for that? Even corrupt tax collectors do that much. If you are kind only to your friends, how are you different from anyone else? Even pagans do that. But you are to be perfect, even as your Father in heaven is perfect."

Forgiveness Matters
Matthew 6:14-15

"If you forgive those who sin against you, your heavenly Father will forgive you. But if you refuse to forgive others, your Father will not forgive your sins."

> *Though your sins are like scarlet, I will make them as white as snow. Though they are red like crimson, I will make them as white as wool.*
> —*Isaiah 1:18*

Pay It Forward
Matthew 18:21-35

Peter came to [Jesus] and asked, "Lord, how often should I forgive someone who sins against me? Seven times?"

"No, not seven times," Jesus replied, "but seventy times seven! "Therefore, the Kingdom of Heaven can be compared to a king who decided to bring his accounts up to date with servants who had borrowed money from him. In the process, one of his debtors was brought in who owed him millions of dollars. He couldn't pay, so his master ordered that he be sold—along with his wife, his children, and everything he owned—to pay the debt.

"But the man fell down before his master and begged him, 'Please, be patient with me, and I will pay it all.' Then his master was filled with pity for him, and he released him and forgave his debt.

"But when the man left the king, he went to a fellow servant who owed him a few thousand dollars. He grabbed him by the throat and demanded instant payment.

"His fellow servant fell down before him and begged for a little more time. 'Be patient with me, and I will pay it,' he pleaded. But his creditor wouldn't wait. He had the man arrested and put in prison until the debt could be paid in full.

"When some of the other servants saw this, they were very upset. They went to the king and told him everything that had happened. Then the king called in the man he had forgiven and said, 'You evil servant! I forgave you that tremendous debt because you pleaded with me. Shouldn't you have mercy on your fellow servant, just as I had mercy on you?' Then the angry king sent the man to prison to be tortured until he had paid his entire debt.

"That's what my heavenly Father will do to you if you refuse to forgive your brothers and sisters from your heart."

We tend to think we deserve forgiveness from pretty much everyone— God and everybody else in our world. We think our friends should not hold a grudge against us and they should never, ever try to get even when we've hurt them. Forgive— that's the way to go. After all, that's what Jesus taught. He said to forgive everyone—even our enemies! But we can't miss the rest of Jesus' teachings about forgiveness. This is important: it goes both ways. Yeah, if you want to be forgiven, you have to be willing to forgive others—even if it is hard. God will help you forgive—and really mean it—if you ask him. If you aren't willing to forgive, like the man in Jesus' story, how can you expect someone else to forgive you? Granted, the whole business of forgiving people (who may not even be sorry for their actions) is not easy, and it's certainly no fun. But when you forgive, it shows your heart truly belongs to God. Ask God to help you with this whole forgiveness thing . . . and thank him for forgiving you!

> **If we confess our sins to him, he is faithful and just to forgive us our sins and to cleanse us from all wickedness.**
>
> **—1 John 1:9**

Friendship

Friends make life a lot more fun, don't they? So how does a person become a friend, anyway? Well, it takes time. First you get to know a person, then you find out what interests you have in common and spend time together, and before you know it, your friendship is cemented and you care about each other. Jesus had some things to say about friendship—especially about how to treat your friends.

Holding Your Friends Accountable
Matthew 18:15-20

"If another believer sins against you, go privately and point out the offense. If the other person listens and confesses it, you have won that person back. But if you are unsuccessful, take one or two others with you and go back again, so that everything you say may be confirmed by two or three witnesses. If the person still refuses to listen, take your case to the church. Then if he or she won't accept the church's decision, treat that person as a pagan or a corrupt tax collector.

"I tell you the truth, whatever you forbid on earth will be forbidden in heaven, and whatever you permit on earth will be permitted in heaven.

"I also tell you this: If two of you agree here on earth concerning anything you ask, my Father in heaven will do it for you. For where two or three gather together as my followers, I am there among them."

Holding Yourself Accountable
Luke 6:37-42

"Do not judge others, and you will not be judged. Do not condemn others, or it will all come back against you. Forgive others, and you will be forgiven. Give, and you will receive. Your gift will return to you in full—pressed down, shaken together to make room for more, running over, and poured into your lap. The amount you give will determine the amount you get back."

> *As iron sharpens iron, so a friend sharpens a friend.*
> —*Proverbs 27:17*

Then Jesus gave the following illustration: "Can one blind person lead another? Won't they both fall into a ditch? Students are not greater than their teacher. But the student who is fully trained will become like the teacher.

"And why worry about a speck in your friend's eye when you have a log in your own? How can you think of saying, 'Friend, let me help you get rid of that speck in your eye,' when you can't see past the log in your own eye? Hypocrite! First get rid of the log in your own eye; then you will see well enough to deal with the speck in your friend's eye."

You Are Jesus' Friend
John 15:9-17

"I have loved you even as the Father has loved me. Remain in my love. When you obey my commandments, you remain in my love, just as I obey my Father's commandments and remain in his love. I have told you these things so that you will be filled with my joy. Yes, your joy will overflow! This is my commandment: Love each other in the same way I have loved you. There is no greater love than to lay down one's life for one's friends. You are my friends if you do what I command. I no longer call you slaves, because a master doesn't confide in his slaves. Now you are my friends, since I have told you everything the

Friendship

Father told me. You didn't choose me. I chose you. I appointed you to go and produce lasting fruit, so that the Father will give you whatever you ask for, using my name. This is my command: Love each other."

One of the most important things about true friendship is honesty. Imagine that a problem develops between you and a good friend and you end up getting really ticked at your friend. Now, you could just

start ignoring that friend and refuse to talk to her or him. At the same time you could start bad-mouthing your friend to others. In the process, you would be wrecking your friend's reputation and pretty much ruining the chance of repairing your friendship. Is that what you really want? You sure wouldn't want someone to do that to you. So Jesus says the way to handle problems is to go to your friend and talk about it—be honest. Hold yourself to the same standard you hold your friends to. That means not criticizing and complaining when your friends do the same things you do. It means correcting your own behavior before you even think about ripping on someone else's actions. In other words, treat others the way you would like to be treated yourself.

A friend is always loyal, and a brother is born to help in time of need.

—Proverbs 17:17

The best thing about friendship, though, is that Jesus is the perfect friend! So if you need ideas about how to treat your friends, you can read about Jesus and how he treated the people around him. Thank God for your friends—and for his friendship with you!

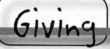

When someone mentions giving, do you automatically think about the wad of cash (or lack of it) in your pocket? Maybe giving is something you hear a lot about in church or youth group, or maybe you hear about it from different organizations that are asking for donations. But in reality, while giving to God's work does involve money, it's also about a lot more than just cash.

G

The Widow's Gift
Mark 12:41-44

Jesus sat down near the collection box in the Temple and watched as the crowds dropped in their money. Many rich people put in large amounts. Then a poor widow came and dropped in two small coins.

Jesus called his disciples to him and said, "I tell you the truth, this poor widow has given more than all the others who are making contributions. For they gave a tiny part of their surplus, but she, poor as she is, has given everything she had to live on."

God's Generosity
Matthew 7:7-11

"Keep on asking, and you will receive what you ask for. Keep on seeking, and you will find. Keep on knocking, and the door will be opened to you. For everyone who asks, receives. Everyone who seeks, finds. And to everyone who knocks, the door will be opened.

Giving

"You parents—if your children ask for a loaf of bread, do you give them a stone instead? Or if they ask for a fish, do you give them a snake? Of course not! So if you sinful people know how to give good gifts to your children, how much more will your heavenly Father give good gifts to those who ask him."

Give with a Clean Heart
Matthew 5:23-24

"If you are presenting a sacrifice at the altar in the Temple and you suddenly remember that someone has something against you, leave your sacrifice there at the altar. Go and be reconciled to that person. Then come and offer your sacrifice to God."

Here's the bottom line: giving, as with pretty much all of the Christian life, starts in the heart. For example, the widow who only had two coins willingly gave all she had to the Lord's work, even though she might not have known where her next meal was coming from. Her heart attitude was so generous and God-focused that she was moved to give everything she had to him. The lesson here is that you can give generously, no matter what finances you've been given.

But there is another kind of offering too—it is the offering of yourself. That means giving your time and abilities to help others. Maybe that means volunteering at a food pantry or working in the nursery at your

---

"Bring all the tithes into the storehouse so there will be enough food in my Temple. If you do," says the LORD of Heaven's Armies, "I will open the windows of heaven for you. I will pour out a blessing so great you won't have enough room to take it in. Try it! Put me to the test!"
—Malachi 3:10

> *God has given each of you a gift from his great variety of spiritual gifts. Use them well to serve one another.*
>
> —1 Peter 4:10

church or tutoring students who need help with English. You can also use special talents God has given you, such as playing a musical instrument, building things, working with technology, acting, or painting, as a way to give.

Now there is one other important thing to understand about giving. Jesus said that if you know some-one is upset with you—if you have offended or hurt someone—you need to settle that before you give. In other words, clean up your heart before you bring an offering to God and ask him to use it and bless it. It's a privilege to be able to give offerings of your time, talents, and money to God. In fact, it's actually a form of worship, so don't take it lightly. Give as generously as you can, and give with a clean heart.

G

Did you know that everything you do—every choice you make, every word you speak, every action you take—shows what you think about God? Hold on . . . don't blow past that statement. Stop and think about it. You can say that you believe in God and that you want to live for him when you're in church or youth group. But it's your whole life that shows how you actually feel about him.

G

God's Blessings
Matthew 5:3-12

"God blesses those who are poor and realize their need for him,
for the Kingdom of Heaven is theirs.

God blesses those who mourn,
for they will be comforted.

God blesses those who are humble,
for they will inherit the whole earth.

God blesses those who hunger and thirst
for justice, for they will be satisfied.

God blesses those who are merciful,
for they will be shown mercy.

God blesses those whose hearts are pure,
for they will see God.

God blesses those who work for peace,
for they will be called the children of God.

God blesses those who are persecuted for doing right,
for the Kingdom of Heaven is theirs.

> *You must love the LORD your God with all your heart, all your soul, and all your strength.*
>
> *—Deuteronomy 6:5*

44

"God blesses you when people mock you and persecute you and lie about you and say all sorts of evil things against you because you are my followers. Be happy about it! Be very glad! For a great reward awaits you in heaven. And remember, the ancient prophets were persecuted in the same way."

Love, Love, Love
Mark 12:28-34

One of the teachers of religious law was standing there listening to the debate. He realized that Jesus had answered well, so he asked, "Of all the commandments, which is the most important?"

Jesus replied, "The most important commandment is this: 'Listen, O Israel! The LORD our God is the one and only LORD. And you must love the LORD your God with all your heart, all your soul, all your mind, and all your strength.' The second is equally important: 'Love your neighbor as yourself.' No other commandment is greater than these."

> *God loved the world so much that he gave his one and only Son, so that everyone who believes in him will not perish but have eternal life.*
>
> —*John 3:16*

The teacher of religious law replied, "Well said, Teacher. You have spoken the truth by saying that there is only one God and no other. And I know it is important to love him with all my heart and all my understanding and all my strength, and to love my neighbor as myself. This is more important than to offer all of the burnt offerings and sacrifices required in the law."

Realizing how much the man understood, Jesus said to him, "You are not far from the Kingdom of God." And after that, no one dared to ask him any more questions.

Jesus Honors God
John 5:19-30

Jesus explained, "I tell you the truth, the Son can do nothing by himself. He does only what he sees the Father doing. Whatever the Father does, the Son also does. For the Father loves the Son and shows him everything he is doing. In fact, the Father will show him how to do even greater works than healing this man. Then you will truly be astonished. For just as the Father gives life to those he raises from the dead, so the Son gives life to anyone he wants. In addition, the Father judges no one. Instead, he has given the Son absolute authority to judge, so that everyone will honor the Son, just as they honor the Father. Anyone who does not honor the Son is certainly not honoring the Father who sent him.

"I tell you the truth, those who listen to my message and believe in God who sent me have eternal life. They will never be condemned for their sins, but they have already passed from death into life.

"And I assure you that the time is coming, indeed it's here now, when the dead will hear my voice—the voice of the Son of God. And those who listen will live. The Father has life in himself, and he has granted that same life-giving power to his Son. And he has given him authority to judge everyone because he is the Son of Man. Don't be so surprised! Indeed, the time is coming when all the dead in their graves will hear the voice of God's Son, and they will rise again. Those who have done good will rise to experience eternal life, and those who have continued in evil will rise to experience judgment. I can do nothing on my own. I judge as God tells me. Therefore, my judgment is just, because I carry out the will of the one who sent me, not my own will."

God is God. He made everything there is. He decides what is right and wrong. And he gets to make the rules. But that's not all. . . . He loves you. He says it over and over in his Word. He shows it every day by what he does for you . . . starting all the way back when he made the world. He made you, too. And he sent Jesus to earth to pay for your sins. Yeah, he loves you. What does he ask for in return? Your love and obedience to him. God knows that life is going to be pretty stinky sometimes. But he promises that if you stay true to him (even in the hard times), he will take care of you. He asks you to love him with all your heart, mind, soul, and strength. Deep love like that will show in your words and actions. It will show in how you treat people around you. God promises to help you with all this. His strength is inside you, and he will help you make decisions, obey him, and love him. It is not a sign of weakness that you need his help—God helped Jesus as he worked on earth too. The bottom line is that God loves you more than you can ever imagine, and he wants your love in return.

G

Grief

Grief hurts. There are times when you're facing a loss and it feels like your heart is breaking. Maybe a loved one has died or a close friend has moved away or you had to let go of something precious to you. There isn't any way around grief. You can pretend that you're just fine, but inside you're a mess. So . . . what do you do about it?

The Promise of New Life
John 5:24-30

"I tell you the truth, those who listen to my message and believe in God who sent me have eternal life. They will never be condemned for their sins, but they have already passed from death into life.

"And I assure you that the time is coming, indeed it's here now, when the dead will hear my voice—the voice of the Son of God. And those who listen will live. The Father has life in himself, and he has granted that same life-giving power to his Son. And he has given him authority to judge everyone because he is the Son of Man. Don't be so surprised! Indeed, the time is coming when all the dead in their graves will hear the voice of God's Son, and they will rise again. Those who have done good will rise to experience eternal life, and those who have continued in evil will rise to experience judgment. I can do nothing on my own. I judge as God tells me. Therefore, my judgment is just, because I carry out the will of the one who sent me, not my own will."

Give all your worries and cares to God, for he cares about you.

—1 Peter 5:7

Jesus Grieves over His Friend

John 11:17-44

When Jesus arrived at Bethany, he was told that Lazarus had already been in his grave for four days. Bethany was only a few miles down the road from Jerusalem, and many of the people had come to console Martha and Mary in their loss. When Martha got word that Jesus was coming, she went to meet him. But Mary stayed in the house.

Martha said to Jesus, "Lord, if only you had been here, my brother would not have died. But even now I know that God will give you whatever you ask."

Jesus told her, "Your brother will rise again."

"Yes," Martha said, "he will rise when everyone else rises, at the last day."

Jesus told her, "I am the resurrection and the life. Anyone who believes in me will live, even after dying. Everyone who lives in me and believes in me will never ever die. Do you believe this, Martha?"

"Yes, Lord," she told him. "I have always believed you are the Messiah, the Son of God, the one who has come into the world from God." Then she returned to Mary. She called Mary aside from the mourners and told her, "The Teacher is here and wants to see you." So Mary immediately went to him.

Jesus had stayed outside the village, at the place where Martha met him. When the people who were at the house consoling Mary saw her leave so hastily, they assumed she was going to Lazarus's grave to weep. So they followed her there. When Mary arrived and saw Jesus, she fell at his feet and said, "Lord, if only you had been here, my brother would not have died."

When Jesus saw her weeping and saw the other people wailing with her, a deep anger welled up within him, and he was deeply troubled. "Where have you put him?" he asked them.

They told him, "Lord, come and see." Then Jesus wept. The people who were standing nearby said, "See how much he loved him!" But some said, "This man healed a blind man. Couldn't he have kept Lazarus from dying?"

Jesus was still angry as he arrived at the tomb, a cave with a stone rolled across its entrance. "Roll the stone aside," Jesus told them.

But Martha, the dead man's sister, protested, "Lord, he has been dead for four days. The smell will be terrible."

> *Even when I walk through the darkest valley, I will not be afraid, for you are close beside me.*
>
> —Psalm 23:4

Jesus responded, "Didn't I tell you that you would see God's glory if you believe?" So they rolled the stone aside. Then Jesus looked up to heaven and said, "Father, thank you for hearing me. You always hear me, but I said it out

Hatred

loud for the sake of all these people standing here, so that they will believe you sent me." Then Jesus shouted, "Lazarus, come out!" And the dead man came out, his hands and feet bound in graveclothes, his face wrapped in a headcloth. Jesus told them, "Unwrap him and let him go!"

Love and grief are closely related. Does that sound strange at first? Think about it though. You wouldn't grieve over losing someone if you didn't love the person to begin with. So if you have the joy of loving someone, part of it is also accepting the pain of grief that will come at some point in your life. But don't worry—it's worth it. Of course, it's hard to believe that when you're in the middle of crying your eyes out. But no matter how much it hurts, you can be sure that Jesus knows how grief feels. He grieved for his friend Lazarus, and he knows it hurts to lose a loved one. The grief of losing a loved one to death is probably one of the deepest griefs you'll face. What makes it bearable, though, is Jesus' promise of resurrection. Christians who know Jesus are promised that even though they die, they will one day be raised to life again and will be together with their loved ones in heaven. So if you have to say good-bye to someone who dies, go ahead and grieve, because that is normal and healthy. But even in your grief you can have hope in the promise of new life in Christ! In the meantime, reach out to Jesus for comfort and strength to get through the pain. He's been through it. He knows what it's like. And he will help you.

Hatred

Have you ever said, "I hate you!" to someone? Did you really mean it? Probably not. (Hopefully not.) Hatred is a very strong emotion. It's more than just being rude or showing your dislike for another person. It's something that starts

on the inside, in your heart. It's not possible to be living for God and have hatred in your heart for someone else. The two things can't exist together—eventually one will win out over the other.

Loving Your Enemies
Luke 6:27-36

"To you who are willing to listen, I say, love your enemies! Do good to those who hate you. Bless those who curse you. Pray for those who hurt you. If someone slaps you on one cheek, offer the other cheek also. If some-one demands your coat, offer your shirt also. Give to anyone who asks; and when things are taken away from you, don't try to get them back. Do to others as you would like them to do to you.

> *Do not nurse hatred in your heart for any of your relatives. Confront people directly so you will not be held guilty for their sin.*
> —*Leviticus 19:17*

H

"If you love only those who love you, why should you get credit for that? Even sinners love those who love them! And if you do good only to those who do good to you, why should you get credit? Even sinners do that much! And if you lend money only to those who can repay you, why should you get credit? Even sinners will lend to other sinners for a full return.

"Love your enemies! Do good to them. Lend to them without expecting to be repaid. Then your reward from heaven will be very great, and you will truly be acting as children of the Most High, for he is kind to those who are unthankful and wicked. You must be compassionate, just as your Father is compassionate."

Hating the Dark Side
Luke 16:13

"No one can serve two masters. For you will hate one and love the other; you will be devoted to one and despise the other. You cannot serve both God and money."

Being Hated for Jesus' Sake
John 15:18-27

"If the world hates you, remember that it hated me first. The world would love you as one of its own if you belonged to it, but you are no longer part of the world. I chose you to come out of the world, so it hates you. Do you remember what I told you? 'A slave is not greater than the master.' Since they persecuted me, naturally they will persecute you. And if they had listened to me, they would listen to you. They will do all this to you because of me, for they have rejected the One who sent me. They would not be guilty if I had not come and spoken to them. But now they have no excuse for their sin. Anyone who hates me also hates my Father. If I hadn't done such miraculous signs among them that no one else could do, they would not be guilty. But as it is, they have seen everything I did, yet they still hate me and my Father. This fulfills what is written in their Scriptures: 'They hated me without cause.'

"But I will send you the Advocate—the Spirit of truth. He will come to you from the Father and will testify all about me. And you must also testify about me because you have been with me from the beginning of my ministry."

If someone says, "I love God," but hates a Christian brother or sister, that person is a liar; for if we don't love people we can see, how can we love God, whom we cannot see?
—1 John 4:20

Whether you like it or not, how you feel about other people is important to Jesus. He taught that the second greatest commandment is to love your neighbor as much as you love yourself. God's Word says that people will know you are a follower of his if you love other people— even your enemies. Yikes. That's not easy, is it? But when you think about it, lots of people can love their friends, whether they have God's strength in them or not. Loving the

H

people who are not very lovable is what sets God's followers apart. That doesn't mean that if a person does something terrible, hurtful, or wrong you have to love those things. Nope, you can hate their actions but still love the person . . . with God's love.

The other thing Jesus said about hatred involves what is important to you. The thing is, at some point in your life you have to make a choice. Some people try to follow God only halfway. With one part of their hearts they want to be committed to Jesus, but the other part is committed to another master, whether it's money or popularity or a certain relationship. When you're trying to straddle the fence between two things, Jesus says you will end up hating one of them and loving the other. Make a choice to live your life for God no matter what, even if it means being hated for it. Wow, that's harsh, isn't it? But if you think about it, some people disliked Jesus so much that they had him killed. So if you follow God, it only makes sense that some people will hate you for that. But still, it's the best place to be, so stay as close to God as you can!

H

Heaven

What do you imagine heaven will be like? Do you picture a misty, cloudy place where everything is white and clean? Do you imagine that soft music plays all the time? Or maybe you're fascinated by some of the descriptions in the book of Revelation about the streets of gold and all that. If you believe that Jesus is the way, the truth, and the life, then heaven is definitely in your future. Let's see what Jesus said about it.

The Narrow Way
Matthew 7:13-14

"You can enter God's Kingdom only through the narrow gate. The highway to hell is broad, and its gate is wide for the many who choose that way. But the gateway to life is very narrow and the road is difficult, and only a few ever find it."

Comfort in Heaven
Luke 16:19-31

Jesus said, "There was a certain rich man who was splendidly clothed in purple and fine linen and who lived each day in luxury. At his gate lay a poor man named Lazarus who was covered with sores. As Lazarus lay there longing for scraps from the rich man's table, the dogs would come and lick his open sores.

> *That is what the Scriptures mean when they say, "No eye has seen, no ear has heard, and no mind has imagined what God has prepared for those who love him."*
>
> *—1 Corinthians 2:9*

H

> *All who are victorious will be clothed in white. I will never erase their names from the Book of Life, but I will announce before my Father and his angels that they are mine.*
>
> *—Revelation 3:5*

"Finally, the poor man died and was carried by the angels to be with Abraham. The rich man also died and was buried, and his soul went to the place of the dead. There, in torment, he saw Abraham in the far distance with Lazarus at his side.

"The rich man shouted, 'Father Abraham, have some pity! Send Lazarus over here to dip the tip of his finger in water and cool my tongue. I am in anguish in these flames.'

"But Abraham said to him, 'Son, remember that during your lifetime you had everything you wanted, and Lazarus had nothing. So now he is here being comforted, and you are in anguish. And besides, there is a great chasm separating us. No one can cross over to you from here, and no one can cross over to us from there.'

H

"Then the rich man said, 'Please, Father Abraham, at least send him to my father's home. For I have five brothers, and I want him to warn them so they don't end up in this place of torment.'

"But Abraham said, 'Moses and the prophets have warned them. Your brothers can read what they wrote.'

"The rich man replied, 'No, Father Abraham! But if someone is sent to them from the dead, then they will repent of their sins and turn to God.'

"But Abraham said, 'If they won't listen to Moses and the prophets, they won't listen even if someone rises from the dead.'"

Jesus Is Preparing a Home For You
John 14:1-7

"Don't let your hearts be troubled. Trust in God, and trust also in me. There is more than enough room in my Father's home. If this were not so, would I have told you that I am going to prepare a place for you? When everything is ready,

Holy Spirit

I will come and get you, so that you will always be with me where I am. And you know the way to where I am going."

"No, we don't know, Lord," Thomas said. "We have no idea where you are going, so how can we know the way?"

Jesus told him, "I am the way, the truth, and the life. No one can come to the Father except through me. If you had really known me, you would know who my Father is. From now on, you do know him and have seen him!"

How cool is this? Jesus himself is preparing your home in heaven. He promised his followers that he would! But not just anybody gets to come. Heaven has a narrow door, and the only way to get through is to ask Jesus to be your Savior. When you do that, the doorway to heaven is opened wide!

Your heavenly family is amazing, too, because it includes people from all over the world who speak every different language. But in heaven we'll all understand each other! The more you find out about heaven, the more you'll want it to be your future. It will become so important that you'll be willing to give up everything else in order to have it.

One thing we know for sure about heaven is that no sin is allowed in. God's Kingdom cannot be contaminated by evil. That's why the doorway to enter is narrow—only those whose sins have been taken away by Christ can come in. Heaven is a place filled with joy, and the rest of eternity will be spent praising and worshiping God there. A lot of the details about heaven are a mystery, but that's okay because you can trust God completely. If he says it's a wonderful place, then it is!

Holy Spirit

The Holy Spirit is kind of hard to understand. He's a part of the Trinity, and he lives inside you. When Jesus went back to heaven, he sent the Holy Spirit to be with Christians. But what does the Holy Spirit actually do? One way to think about him

is that he's like electricity—a power source. He gives you wisdom when you don't know what to do or say. He guides you. He even prays for you when you can't find the words.

The Holy Spirit Speaks for You
Matthew 10:16-20

"Look, I am sending you out as sheep among wolves. So be as shrewd as snakes and harmless as doves. But beware! For you will be handed over to the courts and will be flogged with whips in the synagogues. You will stand trial before governors and kings because you are my followers. But this will be your opportunity to tell the rulers and other unbelievers about me. When you are arrested, don't worry about how to respond or what to say. God will give you the right words at the right time. For it is not you who will be speaking—it will be the Spirit of your Father speaking through you."

> *You will receive power when the Holy Spirit comes upon you. And you will be my witnesses, telling people about me everywhere—in Jerusalem, throughout Judea, in Samaria, and to the ends of the earth.*
>
> *—Acts 1:8*

H

The Holy Spirit Is with You
John 16:5-15

"Now I am going away to the One who sent me, and not one of you is asking where I am going. Instead, you grieve because of what I've told you. But in fact, it is best for you that I go away, because if I don't, the Advocate won't come. If I do go away, then I will send him to you. And when he comes, he will convict the world of its sin, and of God's righteousness, and of the coming judgment. The world's sin is that

Holy Spirit

> *The Holy Spirit helps us in our weakness. For example, we don't know what God wants us to pray for. But the Holy Spirit prays for us with groanings that cannot be expressed in words.*
>
> *—Romans 8:26*

it refuses to believe in me. Righteousness is available because I go to the Father, and you will see me no more. Judgment will come because the ruler of this world has already been judged.

"There is so much more I want to tell you, but you can't bear it now. When the Spirit of truth comes, he will guide you into all truth. He will not speak on his own but will tell you what he has heard. He will tell you about the future. He will bring me glory by telling you whatever he receives from me. All that belongs to the Father is mine; this is why I said, 'The Spirit will tell you whatever he receives from me.'"

The Holy Spirit is an amazing gift to Jesus' followers. He is the third person of the Trinity—God the Father, God the Son, and God the Holy Spirit. Think about this amazing truth—the Holy Spirit lives in you. In you. That means that God is always, constantly with you. Not just with you as in walking along beside you, but inside you giving you power. When you are so tired, sad, or confused that you don't know what to do, the Holy Spirit will give you wisdom. When you don't know what to say, he will give you the right words to speak. How amazing is that? The Holy Spirit also points out your sin and your need for Jesus in your life. And when you simply do not know how to pray—when you can't even come up with the words to say—he will pray on your behalf. That's how much he loves you!

The Spirit has several names throughout Scripture. He is called a helper, a comforter, an encourager, and a counselor. He helps you when you face temptation. He comforts you when you're sad. He encourages you to become the person God wants you to be. He gives you wisdom in making decisions. Because he is in you, you have a job to do—sharing the gospel message with the rest of the world. The Holy Spirit is God . . . alive in you!

Honesty

Do you consider yourself to be an honest person? Most people do. Some people even think, Hey, I'm honest with the big stuff, but if I tell a few white lies here and there, no big deal, right? *Wrong. You may not realize it, but dishonesty always hurts someone, and sometimes that person is you.*

H

Honesty Will Show
Matthew 12:33-36

"A tree is identified by its fruit. If a tree is good, its fruit will be good. If a tree is bad, its fruit will be bad. You brood of snakes! How could evil men like you speak what is good and right? For whatever is in your heart determines what you say. A good person produces good things from the treasury of a good heart, and an evil person produces evil things from the treasury of an evil heart. And I tell you this, you must give an account on judgment day for every idle word you speak."

Who may climb the mountain of the LORD? Who may stand in his holy place? Only those whose hands and hearts are pure, who do not worship idols and never tell lies.

—*Psalm 24:3-4*

59

Honesty Is More than Words
Mark 12:35-40

As Jesus was teaching the people in the Temple, he asked, "Why do the teachers of religious law claim that the Messiah is the son of David? For David himself, speaking under the inspiration of the Holy Spirit, said,

> 'The LORD said to my Lord,
> Sit in the place of honor at my right hand
> until I humble your enemies beneath your feet.'

> *Honesty guides good people; dishonesty destroys treacherous people.*
> —*Proverbs 11:3*

Since David himself called the Messiah 'my Lord,' how can the Messiah be his son?" The large crowd listened to him with great delight.

Jesus also taught: "Beware of these teachers of religious law! For they like to parade around in flowing robes and receive respectful greetings as they walk in the marketplaces. And how they love the seats of honor in the synagogues and the head table at banquets. Yet they shamelessly cheat widows out of their property and then pretend to be pious by making long prayers in public. Because of this, they will be more severely punished."

Honesty Grows Trust
Luke 16:1-12

Jesus told this story to his disciples: "There was a certain rich man who had a manager handling his affairs. One day a report came that the manager was wasting his employer's money. So the employer called him in and said, 'What's this I hear about you? Get your report in order, because you are going to be fired.'

"The manager thought to himself, 'Now what? My boss has fired me. I don't have the strength to dig ditches, and I'm too proud to beg. Ah, I know how to ensure that I'll have plenty of friends who will give me a home when I am fired.'

"So he invited each person who owed money to his employer to come and discuss the situation. He asked the first one, 'How much do you owe him?' The man replied, 'I owe him 800 gallons of olive oil.' So the manager told him, 'Take the bill and quickly change it to 400 gallons.'

"'And how much do you owe my employer?' he asked the next man. 'I owe him 1,000 bushels of wheat,' was the reply. 'Here,' the manager said, 'take the bill and change it to 800 bushels.'

"The rich man had to admire the dishonest rascal for being so shrewd. And it is true that the children of this world are more shrewd in dealing with the world around them than are the children of the light. Here's the lesson: Use your worldly resources to benefit others and make friends. Then, when your earthly possessions are gone, they will welcome you to an eternal home.

"If you are faithful in little things, you will be faithful in large ones. But if you are dishonest in little things, you won't be honest with greater responsibilities. And if you are untrustworthy about worldly wealth, who will trust you with the true riches of heaven? And if you are not faithful with other people's things, why should you be trusted with things of your own?"

H

The choice to be someone who is honest in all things makes a big statement about your true character. Just as Jesus said, "If you are faithful in little things, you will be faithful in large ones." If you prove that you can be trusted to make honest decisions in small things, then those in authority over you will gradually trust you with greater responsibility. Show your parents that you can be trusted with small acts of obedience, and they will begin to trust you more and more. You can say all the right words to make it sound as though you are honest and you care about others, but your actions have to back that up. The real you will always show through. The choice to be honest no matter what shows that deep inside, you care about other people, because dishonesty or cheating always hurts someone.

Humility

What does the Bible mean when it talks about dishonest actions? Here are a few: stealing from a store, accepting too much change when you buy something, downloading a song you didn't pay for, cheating at a game, looking at someone else's test answers, lying about another person, lying about your own actions. Of course, this list could go on and on, but you get the idea.

If you're honest, you care about other people's reputations (so you won't tell lies about them). If you're honest, you care about what is fair (so you won't cheat on schoolwork). If you're honest, you care about the well-being of others and you respect their hard work (so you won't steal what belongs to someone else). Jesus said that your actions show what is in your heart (like a tree is known by its fruit). If Jesus is in your heart, then his love will show through in your actions.

H

Humility

Here's a news flash: life is not all about you! That comes as a shock for a lot of us. No doubt you're tempted to think that you are the smartest, most interesting, most important person in the world. And pretty soon you start feeling like everyone else is a level below you. That is the opposite of humility. The flip side of humility is pride, and it's not pretty. Jesus had a lot to say about that.

> *God opposes the proud but favors the humble.*
>
> *—James 4:6*

Be like a Child
Matthew 18:2-6

Jesus called a little child to him and put the child among them. Then he said, "I tell you the truth, unless you turn from your sins and become like little children, you will never get into the Kingdom

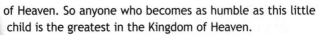

of Heaven. So anyone who becomes as humble as this little child is the greatest in the Kingdom of Heaven.

"And anyone who welcomes a little child like this on my behalf is welcoming me. But if you cause one of these little ones who trusts in me to fall into sin, it would be better for you to have a large millstone tied around your neck and be drowned in the depths of the sea."

Choose Second Place
Luke 14:7-11

When Jesus noticed that all who had come to the dinner were trying to sit in the seats of honor near the head of the table, he gave them this advice: "When you are invited to a wedding feast, don't sit in the seat of honor. What if someone who is more distinguished than you has also been invited? The host will come and say, 'Give this person your seat.' Then you will be embarrassed, and you will have to take whatever seat is left at the foot of the table!

"Instead, take the lowest place at the foot of the table. Then when your host sees you, he will come and say, 'Friend, we have a better place for you!' Then you will be honored in front of all the other guests. For those who exalt themselves will be humbled, and those who humble themselves will be exalted."

Don't Be Proud
Luke 18:9-14

Jesus told this story to some who had great confidence in their own righteousness and scorned everyone else: "Two men went to the Temple to pray. One was a Pharisee, and the other was a despised tax collector. The Pharisee stood by himself and prayed this prayer: 'I thank you, God, that I am not a sinner like everyone else. For I don't cheat, I don't sin, and I don't commit adultery. I'm certainly not like that tax collector! I fast twice a week, and I give you a tenth of my income.'

"But the tax collector stood at a distance and dared not even lift his eyes to heaven as he prayed. Instead, he beat his chest in sorrow, saying, 'O God, be merciful to me, for I am a sinner.' I tell you, this sinner, not the Pharisee, returned home justified before God. For those who exalt themselves will be

Humility

humbled, and those who humble themselves will be exalted."

In our world, pride is often seen as a good thing, or at least a necessary thing. But in Jesus' teachings, there is just no place where pride is valued over humility. Think about it . . . he told grown men and women that they must become like little children to be welcomed into heaven. Not powerful preachers or world leaders or famous celebrities . . . little children.

H *Jesus always modeled humility. Philippians 2:6-7 says that even though Jesus was God, he gave up his privileges as God to take the humble position of being a human. He was the Son of God, but he never acted like he was more important than other people. He talked to the people his society considered worthless. He invited hated tax collectors and uneducated fishermen to be his followers. The call to be humble grows out of Jesus' teaching to love other people as you love yourself. If you do that, then you can cheer for a friend who makes the team when you don't and be glad for the person who gets the solo you wanted in the*

Always be humble and gentle. Be patient with each other, making allowance for each other's faults because of your love.

—Ephesians 4:2

upcoming concert. Humble people celebrate others' successes. They are willing to stay in the background and encourage others to move into the spotlight. The bottom line is that if you're a humble person, you know life is not all about you. You live out Jesus' instructions to love others as you love yourself.

So much of the Christian life is about loving others, lifting them up, encouraging them, celebrating them. This doesn't mean that you should ignore your own self-worth. God made you unique and special . . . but he did that for others, too. All people have value in his sight, so be careful not to elevate yourself above others. Recognize your value to God, and celebrate the value in others, too!

Do you enjoy acting? Sometimes acting like someone
or something different
from what you are is fun . . .
when you're just playing around. But it
can get out of hand when people pretend to be something they aren't just to
impress others. That's called being a hypocrite, and that's serious trouble. Jesus
had a few things to say about hypocrisy.

H

Showing Off
Matthew 6:1-4

"Watch out! Don't do your good
deeds publicly, to be admired by
others, for you will lose the reward from your
Father in heaven. When you give to someone in
need, don't do as the hypocrites do—blowing trumpets in the synagogues and streets to call attention to
their acts of charity! I tell you the truth, they have received
all the reward they will ever get. But when you give to someone in
need, don't let your left hand know what your right hand is doing. Give your
gifts in private, and your Father, who sees everything, will reward you."

Matching Your Walk with Your Talk
Matthew 15:1-9

Some Pharisees and teachers of religious law now arrived from Jerusalem to see
Jesus. They asked him, "Why do your disciples disobey our age-old tradition?
For they ignore our tradition of ceremonial hand washing before they eat."

Jesus replied, "And why do you, by your traditions, violate the direct commandments of God? For instance, God says, 'Honor your father and mother,' and

Hypocrisy

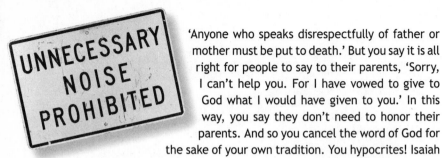

'Anyone who speaks disrespectfully of father or mother must be put to death.' But you say it is all right for people to say to their parents, 'Sorry, I can't help you. For I have vowed to give to God what I would have given to you.' In this way, you say they don't need to honor their parents. And so you cancel the word of God for the sake of your own tradition. You hypocrites! Isaiah was right when he prophesied about you, for he wrote,

'These people honor me with their lips,
but their hearts are far from me.
Their worship is a farce,
for they teach man-made ideas as commands from God.'"

Deal with Yourself
Luke 6:39-42

Jesus gave the following illustration: "Can one blind person lead another? Won't they both fall into a ditch? Students are not greater than their teacher. But the student who is fully trained will become like the teacher.

"And why worry about a speck in your friend's eye when you have a log in your own? How can you think of saying, 'Friend, let me help you get rid of that speck in your eye,' when you can't see past the log in your own eye? Hypocrite! First get rid of the log in your own eye; then you will see well enough to deal with the speck in your friend's eye."

These are just a few examples of what Jesus said about hypocrisy—as you can tell, he had some pretty strong feelings about it. He encouraged people to be honest and real and to live in a way that matched what they said. When Jesus was on earth he often talked to the Pharisees—people who considered themselves super religious. These guys made up a lot of rules about how people should live, and then they judged other people by their rules. But when Jesus looked at them, he saw that they were way more concerned about legalistically following strict rules than about

> **Get rid of all evil behavior. Be done with all deceit, hypocrisy, jealousy, and all unkind speech.**
>
> **—1 Peter 2:1**

what was in their hearts. They worried about little problems other people had but ignored their own giant sins. He warned them to take care of their own sins before they went and criticized someone else's. You're responsible for you!

Jesus also had something to say about people who showed off by doing good things only when other people could see their actions. They were not serious about helping others or showing God's love. They were just showing off to make others think they were super religious, but their hearts weren't interested in serving God. They were hypocrites who wanted people to think they were something they really weren't. You may be able to pretend to be a super Christian who obeys and honors God and fool all the people around you . . . but you won't fool God. Don't waste your energy pretending—be honest with yourself, with others, and with God.

J

> A peaceful heart leads to a healthy body; jealousy is like cancer in the bones.
> —Proverbs 14:30

The green-eyed monster. That's what jealousy is sometimes called. It's a monster because it sneaks up on you and just kind of hijacks your thoughts and actions. It's green because . . . well, who knows why. The important thing to realize is that jealousy can royally mess up relationships. It's *hard to be friends with people you're jealous of—or even to be kind to them. That makes jealousy a big deal.*

Jealousy Comes From Inside
Mark 7:17-23

Jesus went into a house to get away from the crowd, and his disciples asked him what he meant by the parable he had just used. "Don't you understand either?" he asked. "Can't you see that the food you put into your body cannot defile you? Food doesn't go into your heart, but only passes through the stomach and then goes into the sewer." (By saying this, he declared that every kind of food is acceptable in God's eyes.)

> **Thieves are jealous of each other's loot, but the godly are well rooted and bear their own fruit.**
>
> **—Proverbs 12:12**

And then he added, "It is what comes from inside that defiles you. For from within, out of a person's heart, come evil thoughts, sexual immorality, theft, murder, adultery, greed, wickedness, deceit, lustful desires, envy, slander, pride, and foolishness. All these vile things come from within; they are what defile you."

Worrying about the Other Guy
Matthew 20:1-16

"The Kingdom of Heaven is like the land-owner who went out early one morning to hire workers for his vineyard. He agreed to pay the normal daily wage and sent them out to work.

"At nine o'clock in the morning he was passing through the marketplace and saw some people standing around doing nothing. So he hired them, telling them he would pay them whatever was right at the end of the day. So they went to work in the vineyard. At noon and again at three o'clock he did the same thing.

"At five o'clock that afternoon he was in town again and saw some more people standing around. He asked them, 'Why haven't you been working today?'

"They replied, 'Because no one hired us.'

"The landowner told them, 'Then go out and join the others in my vineyard.'

"That evening he told the foreman to call the workers in and pay them, beginning with the last workers first. When those hired at five o'clock were paid, each received a full day's wage. When those hired first came to get their pay, they assumed they would receive more. But they, too, were paid a day's wage. When they received their pay, they protested to the owner, 'Those people worked only one hour, and yet you've paid them just as much as you paid us who worked all day in the scorching heat.'

Most important of all, continue to show deep love for each other, for love covers a multitude of sins.

—1 Peter 4:8

"He answered one of them, 'Friend, I haven't been unfair! Didn't you agree to work all day for the usual wage? Take your money and go. I wanted to pay this last worker the same as you. Is it against the law for me to do what I want with my money? Should you be jealous because I am kind to others?'

"So those who are last now will be first then, and those who are first will be last."

Don't the guys in this story sound like pouty little kids? You don't hear anyone saying, "Thanks for the job and the paycheck." Nope, it's more like, "How come those other guys got as much pay as I did when they didn't work as long?" People who are drowning in jealousy are only

Jesus

concerned about themselves. They don't care a bit about other people's successes, failures, problems, or joys. Nice, huh? Everything is all about them.

What kinds of things can turn normal people into green-eyed monsters? It could be anything, like wanting the stuff your friends have—money, phones, designer clothes, the latest game system—anything. Then there are things like success, popularity, and the desire to become number one in some area. No one is immune to jealousy. A jealous person doesn't usually plan to become that way—it just happens when you let something become so important that you can't think about anything else. It takes over your thoughts and then starts controlling your actions. Getting that thing or achieving that success becomes more important than anything or anyone else. It's not a healthy place to be. Jesus taught that loving him and other people is the most important thing. It's pretty hard to love someone and be jealous of him or her at the same time. You have to dump the green-eyed monster. And the only way to do that is to ask God for his help . . . and his perspective.

J

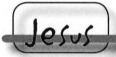

If you've been going to church your whole life, you probably know a lot about Jesus. But do you really know him? He was more than just a historical figure, more than a role model, more than a spiritual leader. Jesus is God's own Son—and God's plan to save people from their sins.

Jesus Is the Bread
John 6:35-38

"I am the bread of life. Whoever comes to me will never be hungry again. Whoever believes in me will never be thirsty.

But you haven't believed in me even though you have seen me. However, those the Father has given me will come to me, and I will never reject them. For I have come down from heaven to do the will of God who sent me, not to do my own will."

Jesus Is the Shepherd
John 10:11-15

"I am the good shepherd. The good shepherd sacrifices his life for the sheep. A hired hand will run when he sees a wolf coming. He will abandon the sheep because they don't belong to him and he isn't their shepherd. And so the wolf attacks them and scatters the flock. The hired hand runs away because he's working only for the money and doesn't really care about the sheep.

J

"I am the good shepherd; I know my own sheep, and they know me, just as my Father knows me and I know the Father. So I sacrifice my life for the sheep."

Jesus Is the True Vine
John 15:1-5

"I am the true grapevine, and my Father is the gardener. He cuts off every branch of mine that doesn't produce fruit, and he prunes the branches that do bear fruit so they will produce even more. You have already been pruned and purified by the message I have given you. Remain in me, and I will remain in you. For a branch cannot produce fruit if it is severed from the vine, and you cannot be fruitful unless you remain in me.

"Yes, I am the vine; you are the branches. Those who remain in me, and I in them, will produce much fruit. For apart from me you can do nothing."

71

Jesus Is the Light
John 8:12-18

"Jesus spoke to the people once more and said, "I am the light of the world. If you follow me, you won't have to walk in darkness, because you will have the light that leads to life."

The Pharisees replied, "You are making those claims about yourself! Such testimony is not valid."

Jesus told them, "These claims are valid even though I make them about myself. For I know where I came from and where I am going, but you don't know this about me. You judge me by human standards, but I do not judge anyone. And if I did, my judgment would be correct in every respect because I am not alone. The Father who sent me is with me. Your own law says that if two people agree about something, their witness is accepted as fact. I am one witness, and my Father who sent me is the other."

> *This is the message of Good News for the people of Israel—that there is peace with God through Jesus Christ, who is Lord of all.*
>
> *—Acts 10:36*

J

Maybe you know some of the basics about Jesus—that he is God's Son, that he came to earth as a baby, that he died on the cross for our sins, and that he rose from the dead and returned to heaven. He is the reason salvation is possible for us. And that's not all there is to the story. During Jesus' three and a half years of ministry on earth, he did a lot of teaching about how we should live for God. He also showed us by the way he lived his life how to treat other people and how to honor God. It's easier to learn something when someone shows you how to do it rather than just telling you to do it, right?

Think about this: Jesus went through temptation, so he knows how that feels. He faced people who didn't like him, so he knows how hard that is. He cared for people who had significant problems. He spent time with people, talking to them, listening to them, loving them, and helping them. What a great example for us! Jesus also made it very clear that believing in him—asking him to take control of your life—is the only way to salvation. He also taught a lot about how we can pray, stay close to him, and read his Word. He

> God promised this Good News long ago through his prophets in the holy Scriptures. The Good News is about his Son. In his earthly life he was born into King David's family line, and he was shown to be the Son of God when he was raised from the dead by the power of the Holy Spirit. He is Jesus Christ our Lord.
> —Romans 1:2-4

wants us to know that the strength to obey God and love others comes from him—the true vine! Stay connected to him, and he will help you with whatever life brings your way.

Judgment

It is easy to tell others what to do, isn't it? Even if we don't say it out loud, we have an opinion about exactly what they're doing wrong. When they don't do what we think they should or if they don't do it the way we think they should, we judge them. The thing about judging others is that we usually hold others to a higher standard than we hold ourselves to. In other words, we have a zillion excuses for why we

> Why do you condemn another believer? Why do you look down on another believer? Remember, we will all stand before the judgment seat of God.
> —Romans 14:10

do what we do, but we don't give others a second chance. But who made us the judge anyway? Those are someone else's shoes to fill. . . .

Judgment

The Just Judge
John 5:26-30

"The Father has life in himself, and he has granted that same life-giving power to his Son. And he has given him authority to judge everyone because he is the Son of Man. Don't be so surprised! Indeed, the time is coming when all the dead in their graves will hear the voice of God's Son, and they will rise again. Those who have done good will rise to experience eternal life, and those who have continued in evil will rise to experience judgment. I can do nothing on my own. I judge as God tells me. Therefore, my judgment is just, because I carry out the will of the one who sent me, not my own will."

Judging Others
Luke 6:37-42

"Do not judge others, and you will not be judged. Do not condemn others, or it will all come back against you. Forgive others, and you will be forgiven. Give, and you will receive. Your gift will return to you in full—pressed down, shaken together to make room for more, running over, and poured into your lap. The amount you give will determine the amount you get back."

Then Jesus gave the following illustration: "Can one blind person lead another? Won't they both fall into a ditch? Students are not greater than their teacher. But the student who is fully trained will become like the teacher.

"And why worry about a speck in your friend's eye when you have a log in your own? How can you think of saying, 'Friend, let me help you get rid of that speck in your eye,' when you can't see past the log in your own eye? Hypocrite! First get rid of the log in your own eye; then you will see well enough to deal with the speck in your friend's eye."

Have you ever said, "Oh, I'm not judging that person—I'm just concerned about them"? Right. Sometimes we pretend to be speaking out of care about someone, but actually all we're doing is judging him or her. After all, if you point out someone else's failures, it makes you look even better, right? It is so easy to judge others—it can happen before you even realize it. You see their failures and problems, and bam, suddenly you're judging them! But if you looked in a mirror, would you see those same kinds of failures in your own life? Probably, and chances are, that's when the "Yeah, buts" begin . . . you know, "Yeah, but I did this because . . ." Any sentence that begins with "Yeah, but" is a dangerous one. Jesus said that the same way you judge other people is the same way you will be judged. Yikes! That makes you want to be a little more careful, doesn't it? The Bible tells us that all of us are sinners. We all fall short of the standard that Jesus set. So just as you cut yourself slack, cut slack for others. Realize that learning to live for Christ is a process. Make it your goal to encourage others in the process rather than judging them.

> **The LORD said to Samuel, "Don't judge by his appearance or height, for I have rejected him. The LORD doesn't see things the way you see them. People judge by outward appearance, but the LORD looks at the heart."**
>
> **—1 Samuel 16:7**

K

The Kingdom of God

Maybe you've heard about the Kingdom of God before, but it's kind of hard to figure out what that Kingdom is like, isn't it? You know that Jesus promised it to believers, but sometimes it's hard to believe it's real, because you can't see a picture of it or hear a report about it from

The Kingdom of God

someone who has been there. But Jesus had a lot to say about it—take a look.

Come like a Child
Matthew 19:13-15

One day some parents brought their children to Jesus so he could lay his hands on them and pray for them. But the disciples scolded the parents for bothering him.

But Jesus said, "Let the children come to me. Don't stop them! For the Kingdom of Heaven belongs to those who are like these children." And he placed his hands on their heads and blessed them before he left.

The Least Will Be the Greatest
Luke 13:23-30

K

Someone asked him, "Lord, will only a few be saved?"

He replied, "Work hard to enter the narrow door to God's Kingdom, for many will try to enter but will fail. When the master of the house has locked the door, it will be too late.

> *You can be sure that no immoral, impure, or greedy person will inherit the Kingdom of Christ and of God. For a greedy person is an idolater, worshiping the things of this world.*
>
> *—Ephesians 5:5*

You will stand outside knocking and pleading, 'Lord, open the door for us!' But he will reply, 'I don't know you or where you come from.' Then you will say, 'But we ate and drank with you, and you taught in our streets.' And he will reply, 'I tell you, I don't know you or where you come from. Get away from me, all you who do evil.'

"There will be weeping and gnashing of teeth, for you will see Abraham, Isaac, Jacob, and all the prophets in the Kingdom of God, but you will be thrown out. And people will come from all over the world—from east and west, north and south—to take their places in the Kingdom of God. And note this: Some who seem least important now will be the greatest then, and some who are the greatest now will be least important then."

You Must Be Born Again
John 3:5-8

"I assure you, no one can enter the Kingdom of God without being born of water and the Spirit. Humans can reproduce only human life, but the Holy Spirit gives birth to spiritual life. So don't be surprised when I say, 'You must be born again.' The wind blows wherever it wants. Just as you can hear the wind but can't tell where it comes from or where it is going, so you can't explain how people are born of the Spirit."

K

The Kingdom of God isn't exactly a place like the kingdoms in our world. It's more like the family you are adopted into when you ask Jesus to be your Savior. Maybe Jesus didn't focus much on the physical place, but he sure had a lot to say about the people in the Kingdom of God. Right off the bat he made it clear that his Kingdom is not just for the rich, famous, or powerful. In fact, he pointed out that the humble and innocent— those who become like children—will be most welcomed in God's Kingdom. People who think a lot of themselves and assume they will have an important place in God's Kingdom are probably just fooling themselves. Over and over again Jesus made the point that pride and an "I'm better than you" attitude have no place in his Kingdom. He even said that people who

Leaders

> *The Kingdom of God is not a matter of what we eat or drink, but of living a life of goodness and peace and joy in the Holy Spirit.*
>
> —Romans 14:17

seem to be nobodies may actually be the greatest in God's Kingdom. That's because God looks at our hearts and sees how much we love him and want to serve him. That's what makes a person great in God's eyes.

If you want to be part of God's Kingdom, you have to know him. Power, money, fame, or parents who know God will not get you into God's Kingdom. The only way in is through Jesus: accepting him as Savior, confessing your sin to him—in other words, becoming born again. This phrase—"born again"—has been interpreted a lot of different ways, but it just means that the dirt of your sins has been washed off and you have become a brand-new person—someone God will welcome into his Kingdom!

L

Leaders

A leader isn't a leader unless people are following. Have you ever found yourself in a leadership position? Many people don't realize that it's a big responsibility to be a leader. Yeah, a leader who doesn't obey God and leads his or her

followers away from God is in big trouble. In God's eyes a real leader is someone who acts with integrity and helps people draw closer to God. Any other kind of leader may actually be more of a bully or a dictator—definitely not the kind of leader God has in mind.

Leadership by Example
Matthew 23:1-12

Jesus said to the crowds and to his disciples, "The teachers of religious law and the Pharisees are the official interpreters of the law of Moses. So practice and obey whatever they tell you, but don't follow their example. For they don't practice what they teach. They crush people with unbearable religious demands and never lift a finger to ease the burden.

"Everything they do is for show. On their arms they wear extra wide prayer boxes with Scripture verses inside, and they wear robes with extra long tassels. And they love to sit at the head table at banquets and in the seats of honor in the synagogues. They love to receive respectful greetings as they walk in the marketplaces, and to be called 'Rabbi.'

"Don't let anyone call you 'Rabbi,' for you have only one teacher, and all of you are equal as brothers and sisters. And don't address anyone here on earth as 'Father,' for only God in heaven is your spiritual Father. And don't let anyone call you 'Teacher,' for you have only one teacher, the Messiah. The greatest among you must be a servant. But those who exalt themselves will be humbled, and those who humble themselves will be exalted."

> *Whoever wants to be a leader among you must be your servant, and whoever wants to be first among you must become your slave. For even the Son of Man came not to be served but to serve others and to give his life as a ransom for many.*
>
> *—Matthew 20:26-28*

L

Servant Leadership
Luke 22:25-27

"In this world the kings and great men lord it over their people, yet they are called 'friends of the people.' But among you it will be different. Those who are the greatest among you should take the lowest rank, and the leader should be like a servant. Who is more important, the one who sits at the table or the one who serves? The one who sits at the table, of course. But not here! For I am among you as one who serves."

Humble Leadership
John 13:12-17

After washing their feet, [Jesus] put on his robe again and sat down and asked, "Do you understand what I was doing? You call me 'Teacher' and 'Lord,' and you are right, because that's what I am. And since I, your Lord and Teacher, have washed your feet, you ought to wash each other's feet. I have given you an example to follow. Do as I have done to you. I tell you the truth, slaves are not greater than their master. Nor is the messenger more important than the one who sends the message. Now that you know these things, God will bless you for doing them."

L

You must have the same attitude that Christ Jesus had. Though he was God, he did not think of equality with God as something to cling to. Instead, he gave up his divine privileges; he took the humble position of a slave and was born as a human being.

—Philippians 2:5-7

Some people want to be leaders because they like the power and they like having others follow them and do what they say. Other people are natural leaders because they make wise choices and others want to follow them. Either way, there is one characteristic of a true leader that may seem a bit strange: a true leader is a servant. What does that mean? When Jesus said that a leader should be a servant, he was making a contrast between real leaders and some of the religious authorities of his day who thought they should have special privileges and be treated with high honors. The show-off leaders wanted people to notice them and make a big deal about them. But Jesus said that real leaders serve other people. They do things for others and look for ways to help them. True leaders help their followers succeed and grow stronger.

Jesus modeled this kind of servant leadership. He didn't ask to have the best seat at dinner parties. He didn't insist on being treated like a celebrity. He constantly looked for ways to help people, even when it wasn't convenient for him and even when he was really tired. Real leaders help their followers know God better and serve him with more energy. If you find yourself in a leadership role, the best thing you can do to be a good leader is to be a good follower . . . of Jesus.

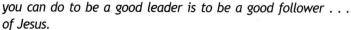

Life

Life can seem overwhelming sometimes. And maybe you've wondered at times if God cares . . . or if he even notices. Does God know what it's like to be human—to be you?

You have been taught the holy Scriptures from childhood, and they have given you the wisdom to receive the salvation that comes by trusting in Christ Jesus.
—2 Timothy 3:15

God Has Things under Control
Luke 12:22-31

Turning to his disciples, Jesus said, "That is why I tell you not to worry about everyday life—whether you have enough food to eat or enough clothes to wear. For life is more than food, and your body more than clothing. Look at the ravens. They don't plant or harvest or store food in barns, for God feeds them. And you are far more valuable to him than any birds! Can all your worries add a single moment to your life? And if worry can't accomplish a little thing like that, what's the use of worrying over bigger things?

"Look at the lilies and how they grow. They don't work or make their clothing, yet Solomon in all his glory was not dressed as beautifully as they are. And if God cares so wonderfully for flowers that are here today and thrown into the fire tomorrow, he will certainly care for you. Why do you have so little faith?

"And don't be concerned about what to eat and what to drink. Don't worry about such things. These things dominate the thoughts of unbelievers all over the world, but your Father already knows your needs. Seek the Kingdom of God above all else, and he will give you everything you need."

A Matter of Life and Death
John 12:23-25

Jesus replied, "Now the time has come for the Son of Man to enter into his glory. I tell you the truth, unless a kernel of wheat is planted in the soil and dies, it remains alone. But its death will produce many new kernels—a plentiful harvest of new lives. Those who love their life in this world will lose it. Those who care nothing for their life in this world will keep it for eternity."

Does it surprise you that Jesus actually talked about clothes and food? He is God, but he is human, too, and he knows what it is like to have earthly, human concerns. He knows that people can easily get caught up in worrying about clothing—about if they have enough money for the basics or if they have the right clothes to wear. But Jesus said that if you're worrying a lot about clothes, you won't have much energy left to think about God. He also said that we don't need to worry about food. Of course, if you're truly hungry, it's hard to think about anything else. But Jesus' point is that worrying about it won't change anything. He pointed out that God takes care of all creation; plants and animals don't even have to think about their needs because God supplies food for them and makes them grow. He will take care of you, too, because he loves you more than you can even imagine.

> *I pray that God, the source of hope, will fill you completely with joy and peace because you trust in him.*
>
> **—Romans 15:13**

Of course your life is important to you—and it should be. You only get one chance at life on this earth, so make the most of your moments here. Don't waste your time worrying about stuff. Spend your energy trusting God and growing your faith in him stronger and stronger. Make your one life on earth count for God!

L

Listening

Are you a good listener? Let's break that down—are you a good listener when your friends have something to say? And are you a good listener when your parents are talking to you or giving you jobs to do? How good of a listener are you when your teacher is explaining things in class? There are all kinds of listening, but Jesus was most concerned about a specific listening ability.

Listen to Each Other
Matthew 18:15-17

"If another believer sins against you, go privately and point out the offense. If the other person listens and confesses it, you have won that person back. But if you are unsuccessful, take one or two others with you and go back again, so that everything you say may be confirmed by two or three witnesses. If the person still refuses to listen, take your case to the church. Then if he or she won't accept the church's decision, treat that person as a pagan or a corrupt tax collector."

Listen to the Shepherd
John 10:1-5

"I tell you the truth, anyone who sneaks over the wall of a sheepfold, rather than going through the gate, must surely be a thief and a robber! But the one who enters through the gate is the shepherd of the sheep. The gatekeeper opens the gate for him, and the sheep recognize his voice and come to him. He calls his own sheep by name and leads them out. After he has gathered his own flock, he walks ahead of them, and they follow him because they know his voice. They won't follow a stranger; they will run from him because they don't know his voice."

The Most Important Thing to Listen To
Luke 8:16-18

"No one lights a lamp and then covers it with a bowl or hides it under a bed. A lamp is placed on a stand, where its light can be seen by all who enter the house. For all that is secret will eventually be brought into the open, and everything that is concealed will be brought to light and made known to all.

"So pay attention to how you hear. To those who listen to my teaching, more understanding will be given. But for those who are not listening, even what they think they understand will be taken away from them."

There's no doubt that Jesus thought listening was important. It's true that he didn't specifically mention listening to instructions about homework or chores. But if you put together the words of Jesus and the teachings from other parts of the Bible, you know that he promotes that kind of listening too. One thing Jesus taught over and over was that people should love one another. That means caring about what others are going through, what they are scared of, and what they are celebrating. You can't know those things if you don't listen! Jesus also talked about the importance of listening to people you aren't getting along with. After all, how can you solve the problem if you don't talk to each other?

Another part of listening that Jesus was concerned about was

> *Too much talk leads to sin. Be sensible and keep your mouth shut.*
> —*Proverbs 10:19*

> *If you reject discipline, you only harm yourself; but if you listen to correction, you grow in understanding.*
> —*Proverbs 15:32*

L

Love

who *you* listen to. Where do you turn for advice or guidance? Jesus warns you to be careful who you listen to, because some people will lead you away from obeying him. Some people spout advice or even "rules" that might sound good but have nothing to do with God or what he thinks. Jesus said that the more you pay attention to his words and his teachings, the more you will understand. Listen more, learn more. Good trade-off, huh?

> Be still, and know that I am God! I will be honored by every nation. I will be honored throughout the world.
> —Psalm 46:10

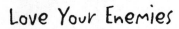

Love

Love . . . blah, blah, blah. If you're a guy, you may be tempted to skip over this section altogether. If you're a girl, you may think about love all the time. Did you know that Jesus had a lot to say about love? Yep, but not so much the mushy, romantic kind of love. The love Jesus taught about isn't always easy, and it definitely takes time. But if you want to know what real love is, take a look at what he had to say about it.

Love Your Enemies
Luke 6:27-36

"To you who are willing to listen, I say, love your enemies! Do good to those who hate you. Bless those who curse you. Pray for those who hurt you. If

someone slaps you on one cheek, offer the other cheek also. If someone demands your coat, offer your shirt also. Give to anyone who asks; and when things are taken away from you, don't try to get them back. Do to others as you would like them to do to you.

"If you love only those who love you, why should you get credit for that? Even sinners love those who love them! And if you do good only to those who do good to you, why should you get credit? Even sinners do that much! And if you lend money only to those who can repay you, why should you get credit? Even sinners will lend to other sinners for a full return.

"Love your enemies! Do good to them. Lend to them without expecting to be repaid. Then your reward from heaven will be very great, and you will truly be acting as children of the Most High, for he is kind to those who are unthankful and wicked. You must be compassionate, just as your Father is compassionate."

> *Dear friends, since God loved us that much, we surely ought to love each other.*
>
> *—1 John 4:11*

L

God's Love
Matthew 18:12-14

"If a man has a hundred sheep and one of them wanders away, what will he do? Won't he leave the ninety-nine others on the hills and go out to search for the one that is lost? And if he finds it, I tell you the truth, he will rejoice over it more than over the ninety-nine that didn't wander away! In the same way, it is not my heavenly Father's will

Love

> *Love is patient and kind.
> Love is not jealous or
> boastful or proud or rude.
> It does not demand its own
> way. It is not irritable, and
> it keeps no record of being
> wronged. It does not rejoice
> about injustice but rejoices
> whenever the truth wins out.
> Love never gives up, never
> loses faith, is always hopeful,
> and endures through every
> circumstance.*
>
> *—1 Corinthians 13:4-7*

that even one of these little ones should perish."

The Most Important Thing
Mark 12:28-34

One of the teachers of religious law was standing there listening to the debate. He realized that Jesus had answered well, so he asked, "Of all the commandments, which is the most important?"

Jesus replied, "The most important commandment is this: 'Listen, O Israel! The LORD our God is the one and only LORD. And you must love the LORD your God with all your heart, all your soul, all your mind, and all your strength.' The second is equally important: 'Love your neighbor as yourself.' No other commandment is greater than these."

The teacher of religious law replied, "Well said, Teacher. You have spoken the truth by saying that there is only one God and no other. And I know it is important to love him with all my heart and all my understanding and all my strength, and to love my neighbor as myself. This is more important than to offer all of the burnt offerings and sacrifices required in the law."

Realizing how much the man understood, Jesus said to him, "You are not far from the Kingdom of God." And after that, no one dared to ask him any more questions.

Real Love
John 15:9-17

"I have loved you even as the Father has loved me. Remain in my love. When you obey my commandments, you remain in my love, just as I obey my Father's commandments and remain in his love. I have told you these things so that you will be filled with my joy. Yes, your joy will overflow!

88

This is my commandment: Love each other in the same way I have loved you. There is no greater love than to lay down one's life for one's friends. You are my friends if you do what I command. I no longer call you slaves, because a master doesn't confide in his slaves. Now you are my friends, since I have told you everything the Father told me. You didn't choose me. I chose you. I appointed you to go and produce lasting fruit, so that the Father will give you whatever you ask for, using my name. This is my command: Love each other."

Love Means Action
John 21:15-19

After breakfast Jesus asked Simon Peter, "Simon son of John, do you love me more than these?"

"Yes, Lord," Peter replied, "you know I love you."

"Then feed my lambs," Jesus told him.

Jesus repeated the question: "Simon son of John, do you love me?"

"Yes, Lord," Peter said, "you know I love you."

"Then take care of my sheep," Jesus said.

L

A third time he asked him, "Simon son of John, do you love me?"

Peter was hurt that Jesus asked the question a third time. He said, "Lord, you know everything. You know that I love you."

Jesus said, "Then feed my sheep.

"I tell you the truth, when you were young, you were able to do as you liked; you dressed yourself and went wherever you wanted to go. But when you are old, you will stretch out your hands, and others will dress you and take you where you don't want to go." Jesus said this to let him know by what kind of death he would glorify God. Then Jesus told him, "Follow me."

Mind

So . . . from Jesus' perspective, love means caring about people who hurt you and don't love you back. God said loving others is one of the most important things—in fact, the only thing more important is loving God himself. Real love means obeying him and serving others. Real love shows itself in action!

Mind

What do you think about most often? Come on, be honest now . . . what runs through your mind every day, maybe even every hour? What takes up most of your mental energy? Well, here's something to think about—the things that occupy your mind are the things that truly matter to you . . . whether you want to admit it or not.

Jesus Can Read Minds
Matthew 9:4-7

Jesus knew what they were thinking, so he asked them, "Why do you have such evil thoughts in your hearts? Is it easier to say 'Your sins are forgiven,' or 'Stand up and walk'? So I will prove to you that the Son of Man has the authority on earth to forgive sins." Then Jesus turned to the paralyzed man and said, "Stand up, pick up your mat, and go home!"

And the man jumped up and went home!

Your Heart Steers Your Mind
Matthew 15:10-20

Jesus called to the crowd to come and hear. "Listen," he said, "and try to understand. It's not what goes into your mouth that defiles you; you are defiled by the words that come out of your mouth."

Then the disciples came to him and asked, "Do you realize you offended the Pharisees by what you just said?"

Jesus replied, "Every plant not planted by my heavenly Father will be uprooted, so ignore them. They are blind guides leading the blind, and if one blind person guides another, they will both fall into a ditch."

Then Peter said to Jesus, "Explain to us the parable that says people aren't defiled by what they eat."

"Don't you understand yet?" Jesus asked. "Anything you eat passes through the stomach and then goes into the sewer. But the words you speak come from the heart—that's what defiles you. For from the heart come evil thoughts, murder, adultery, all sexual immorality, theft, lying, and slander. These are what defile you. Eating with unwashed hands will never defile you."

What makes people say rude, gossipy things? Why do people become super selfish or cheat or tell lies? Well, these things don't happen because of something they ate, that's for sure. Jesus explained where evil stuff starts: in the heart. Yep, selfishness and plain old meanness begin there and then take a quick trip up to the mind. That's where those bad things take root.

> *Don't copy the behavior and customs of this world, but let God transform you into a new person by changing the way you think. Then you will learn to know God's will for you, which is good and pleasing and perfect.*
>
> *—Romans 12:2*

Mind

Once your mind starts thinking only about yourself and how you deserve this or that and you decide that someone is standing in the way of it . . . well, from there, unkind and downright mean words start blasting from your mouth. Next your actions toward others can get really ugly. Sometimes you know your thoughts and actions are taking this downhill path, but even though you want to stop it, you just can't.

> *May all my thoughts be pleasing to him, for I rejoice in the LORD.*
> —Psalm 104:34

Think about it—have you ever felt you got cheated out of something—a place on a team or a certain relationship, for example? Or maybe you think you should have the same stuff that someone else has, and you can't stop thinking about it. Have you ever gotten so consumed by those thoughts that you couldn't think about anything else? Seriously, it's hard to pay attention to anything else when your mind is stuck on one thing . . . and no good is going to come from that. The antidote to this negative thought process is to focus your thoughts on things that are true, honorable, and right. Keep your mind on Jesus and his love.

> *Fix your thoughts on what is true, and honorable, and right, and pure, and lovely, and admirable. Think about things that are excellent and worthy of praise.*
> —Philippians 4:8

Miracles

The word miracle *is used for a lot of things that aren't necessarily miracles. For example, you might say, "It's a miracle that I got an A on that test." Or maybe you've said something like this: "I found my cell phone in the lunchroom trash can. It was a miracle!" Yeah, those things are great . . . but they aren't really miracles. Read about the miracles that Jesus did if you want to know about the real thing!*

The Blind Can See
Matthew 9:27-31

Two blind men followed along behind [Jesus], shouting, "Son of David, have mercy on us!"

They went right into the house where he was staying, and Jesus asked them, "Do you believe I can make you see?"

"Yes, Lord," they told him, "we do."

Then he touched their eyes and said, "Because of your faith, it will happen." Then their eyes were opened, and they could see! Jesus sternly warned them, "Don't tell anyone about this." But instead, they went out and spread his fame all over the region.

M

Miraculous Evidence
Matthew 11:2-6

John the Baptist, who was in prison, heard about all the things the Messiah was doing. So he sent his disciples to ask Jesus, "Are you the Messiah we've been expecting, or should we keep looking for someone else?"

Jesus told them, "Go back to John and tell him what you have heard and seen—the blind see, the lame walk, the lepers are cured, the deaf hear, the dead are raised to life, and the Good News is being preached to the poor. And tell him, 'God blesses those who do not turn away because of me.'"

> *I will meditate on your majestic, glorious splendor and your wonderful miracles.*
>
> *—Psalm 145:5*

Feeding 5,000
Luke 9:12-17

Late in the afternoon the twelve disciples came to him and said, "Send the crowds away to the nearby villages and farms, so they can find food and lodging for the night. There is nothing to eat here in this remote place."

But Jesus replied, "You feed them."

"But we have only five loaves of bread and two fish," they answered. "Or are you expecting us to go and buy enough food for this whole crowd?" For there were about 5,000 men there.

Jesus replied, "Tell them to sit down in groups of about fifty each." So the people all sat down. Jesus took the five loaves and two fish, looked up toward heaven, and blessed them. Then, breaking the loaves into pieces, he kept giving the bread and fish to the disciples so they could distribute it to the people. They all ate as much as they wanted, and afterward, the disciples picked up twelve baskets of leftovers!

> *He alone is your God, the only one who is worthy of your praise, the one who has done these mighty miracles that you have seen with your own eyes.*
>
> *—Deuteronomy 10:21*

A miracle is when something amazing happens and there is no logical explanation for it. It may seem that something like getting an A on a test is a miracle, but true miracles are things like dead people coming back to life or blind people suddenly being able to see. When you read through the Gospels, you come across miracle after miracle—and Jesus was always involved (either in person or through the power he gave his followers).

Why did Jesus do miracles? Well, he cared a lot about people. So when he met people who were sick, hurting, or hungry, he always wanted to do something to help them. The miracles Jesus did showed his amazing power over life, death, health, and everything else. The people around Jesus saw the miracles he did and were amazed. Many of them were moved to believe the truth that he is God's Son and that he has power and strength like no one else. Sometimes people believed; sometimes they did not. But Jesus kept doing miracles, and the most amazing miracle of all was when he himself was raised from the dead. That showed God's power over everything—even death!

Murder

Sometimes when people get really mad at someone they say, "I'm gonna kill you!" Of course, they don't really mean it, but it just shows how casually the topic of murder is treated. If you play video games or watch TV and movies, you've probably seen a bazillion murders! Do you even think about it anymore?

M

Murder Starts in the Heart
Matthew 15:15-20

Peter said to Jesus, "Explain to us the parable that says people aren't defiled by what they eat."

"Don't you understand yet?" Jesus asked. "Anything you eat passes through the stomach and then goes into the sewer. But the words you speak come from the heart—that's what defiles you. For from the heart come evil thoughts, murder, adultery, all sexual immorality, theft, lying, and slander. These are what defile you. Eating with unwashed hands will never defile you."

Are You a Murderer?

Matthew 5:21-24

"You have heard that our ancestors were told, 'You must not murder. If you commit murder, you are subject to judgment.' But I say, if you are even angry with someone, you are subject to judgment! If you call someone an idiot, you are in danger of being brought before the court. And if you curse someone, you are in danger of the fires of hell.

"So if you are presenting a sacrifice at the altar in the Temple and you suddenly remember that someone has something against you, leave your sacrifice there at the altar. Go and be reconciled to that person. Then come and offer your sacrifice to God."

The Father of Murder

John 8:42-45

Jesus told them, "If God were your Father, you would love me, because I have come to you from God. I am not here on my own, but he sent me. Why can't you understand what I am saying? It's because you can't even hear me! For you are the children of your father the devil, and you love to do the evil things he does. He was a murderer from the beginning. He has always hated the truth, because there is no truth in him. When he lies, it is consistent with his character; for he is a liar and the

M

The commandments say, "You must not commit adultery. You must not murder. You must not steal. You must not covet. These—and other such commandments—are summed up in this one commandment: "Love your neighbor as yourself."

—Romans 13:9

father of lies. So when I tell the truth, you just naturally don't believe me!"

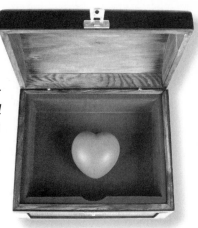

Why does Jesus say that murder starts in the heart? Because the heart is the starting point of all emotions. Anger begins as a feeling and then grows until it becomes a desire—wanting bad things to happen to someone else. Sometimes that desire explodes into action, and the result is murder . . . either literal murder or another hateful action, which God says is just about the same thing.

When two people have some kind of problem, God expects them to talk it out and settle the problem—not to get so angry that it opens the door to murder. Murder is a sin—direct disobedience of God's commands—and Jesus lines it up with Satan himself. There is no way for you to claim you follow God and still

> *Guard your heart above all else, for it determines the course of your life.*
>
> *—Proverbs 4:23*

commit murder—physically or in your heart. Murder, or even deep anger, will always separate you from God. So when you are angry with another person, go talk it out and settle it.

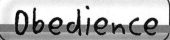

Obedience

O

Obey, obey, obey. Does it make you cringe just to hear the word? Obey your mom. Obey your dad. Obey your teacher. Obey the principal. Obey God. Obey, obey, obey. Have you ever wished for a break from obedience . . . or maybe just a shortcut? Have you ever wondered if it's really that important to always obey? If so, read on. . . .

Obedience Required
Matthew 7:21-23

"Not everyone who calls out to me, 'Lord! Lord!' will enter the Kingdom of Heaven. Only those who actually do the will of my Father in heaven will enter. On judgment day many will say to me, 'Lord! Lord! We prophesied in your name and cast out demons in your name and performed many miracles in your name.' But I will reply, 'I never knew you. Get away from me, you who break God's laws.'"

A Firm Foundation
Luke 6:46-49

"Why do you keep calling me 'Lord, Lord!' when you don't do what I say? I will show you what it's like when someone comes to me, listens to my teaching, and then follows it. It is like a person building a house who digs deep and lays the foundation on solid rock. When the floodwaters rise and break against that house, it stands firm because it is well built. But anyone who hears and doesn't obey is like a person who builds a house without a foundation. When the floods sweep down against that house, it will collapse into a heap of ruins."

O

You were cleansed from your sins when you obeyed the truth, so now you must show sincere love to each other as brothers and sisters. Love each other deeply with all your heart.

—1 Peter 1:22

Love Equals Obedience
John 14:15-17

"If you love me, obey my commandments. And I will ask the Father, and he will give you another Advocate, who will never leave you. He is the Holy Spirit, who leads into all truth. The world cannot receive him, because it isn't looking for him and doesn't recognize him. But you know him, because he lives with you now and later will be in you."

Jesus didn't hold back a bit on this topic—obedience to God is not optional. But Jesus doesn't insist on obedience to God's commands because he is a bully or a control freak. Nope, he expects us to obey because that is the best way to live. He knows that if you obey God's commands you will be happier in the long run. The people around you will be happier too, because obedience means treating them with respect and kindness—loving them as Jesus said to do.

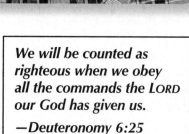

The best way to please God is to obey his commands. In fact, he says that people who claim to love God but don't obey him are just fooling themselves. Love and obedience go together. If you love God, you will serve him more faithfully, pray for others, and read his Word. God didn't make a list of "Do this" and "Don't do that" rules to make your life miserable. His commands are in place to set you free.

> *We will be counted as righteous when we obey all the commands the LORD our God has given us.*
>
> *—Deuteronomy 6:25*

Peace

What comes to mind when you think about peace? Is it just freedom from war? If you are fortunate enough to live in a nation that isn't often at war, maybe the concept of peace doesn't mean much to you. But peace is more than the absence of war. It's also a personal thing . . . like having your own personal sense of calm. If you're at peace, it means you have a quiet and content state of mind—and that's possible whether there's a war going on or not.

Be a Peacemaker
Matthew 5:9

"God blesses those who work for peace, for they will be called the children of God."

Never pay back evil with more evil. Do things in such a way that everyone can see you are honorable. Do all that you can to live in peace with everyone.

—Romans 12:17-18

Blessing of Peace
Luke 10:1-6

The Lord now chose seventy-two other disciples and sent them ahead in pairs to all the towns and places he planned to visit. These were his instructions to them: "The harvest is great, but the workers are few. So pray to the Lord who is in charge of the harvest; ask him to send more workers into his fields. Now go, and remember that I am sending you out as lambs among wolves. Don't take any money with you, nor a traveler's bag, nor an extra pair of sandals. And don't stop to greet anyone on the road.

"Whenever you enter someone's home, first say, 'May God's peace be on this house.' If those who live there are peaceful, the blessing will stand; if they are not, the blessing will return to you."

The Gift Jesus Left

John 14:27-29

"I am leaving you with a gift—peace of mind and heart. And the peace I give is a gift the world cannot give. So don't be troubled or afraid. Remember what I told you: I am going away, but I will come back to you again. If you really loved me, you would be happy that I am going to the Father, who is greater than I am. I have told you these things before they happen so that when they do happen, you will believe."

So where does real peace come from? Not from your circumstances or from sitting in deep meditation or from finding the most relaxing surroundings. True peace can only come from Jesus. He removes worry from your heart. He takes away that struggle inside you to have more stuff and to be more powerful or in control. Those things are the thieves of peace. Jesus will give you true peace—if you let him.

In peace I will lie down and sleep, for you alone, O LORD, will keep me safe.

—Psalm 4:8

P

Peace is important to Jesus. As you read through the stories about the miracles he did, he almost always told the person he had healed or raised back to life to "go in peace." In other words, don't be anxious about how this happened or fight against it—accept it in peace. And where does peace begin? Yep, in the heart. When you ask Jesus into your life, he cleanses your heart of sin and gives you his peace. Then no matter what happens in your life, you can know he is with you giving you his peace—if you will receive it.

Persecution

Jesus also said there is a special blessing for people who spread peace instead of problems. So make an effort to be at peace with others—don't gossip or spread rumors that will cause problems. Don't be a troublemaker. Don't always insist on having your way. Be a person who shares God's peace. Your life will sometimes have problems—you can count on it—because that's just the way life is. But you can also be sure that Jesus' peace is in your heart. So even if things around you aren't quite peaceful, don't worry—know that he is in control and is watching over you.

Persecution

Is there anything you feel strongly enough about that you would take a beating for it . . . or even die for it? That's what persecution is: being abused or pushed around or picked on or physically hurt because of your race, beliefs, religion, or whatever. Most of us have never had to decide if we're willing to physically suffer for what we believe. Did you know, though, that in many parts of the world Christians are persecuted . . . just for believing in Jesus?

Sheep among Wolves
Matthew 10:16-20

"Look, I am sending you out as sheep among wolves. So be as shrewd as snakes and harmless as doves. But beware! For you will be handed over to the courts and will be flogged with whips in the synagogues. You will stand trial before governors and kings because you are my followers. But this will be your opportunity to tell the rulers and other unbelievers about me. When you are arrested, don't worry about how to respond or what to say. God will give you the right words at the right time. For it is not you who will be speaking—it will be the Spirit of your Father speaking through you."

The Good with the Bad
Mark 10:28-31

Peter began to speak up. "We've given up everything to follow you," he said.

"Yes," Jesus replied, "and I assure you that everyone who has given up house or brothers or sisters or mother or father or children or property, for my sake and for the Good News, will receive now in return a hundred times as many houses, brothers, sisters, mothers, children, and property—along with persecution. And in the world to come that person will have eternal life. But many who are the greatest now will be least important then, and those who seem least important now will be the greatest then."

You have been given not only the privilege of trusting in Christ but also the privilege of suffering for him.
—Philippians 1:29

Surprising Blessings
Luke 6:22-23

"What blessings await you when people hate you and exclude you and mock you and curse you as evil because you follow the Son of Man. When that happens, be happy! Yes, leap for joy!

P

Persecution

For a great reward awaits you in heaven. And remember, their ancestors treated the ancient prophets that same way."

Persecution is hard-core bullying. It's an effort to force someone to give up what they believe or at least to pay a high price for their beliefs. Jesus knew that his followers would be persecuted. In fact, he told them to plan on it. He wanted them to be ready to explain why they followed him. He also wanted them to know that if they depended on him, the Holy Spirit would speak through them and they wouldn't have to stress about saying the right things.

Being persecuted for what you believe could mean giving up a lot. Sometimes friends or family members turn against you when you follow Jesus. Some believers lose their popularity, their money, or their reputations. Jesus promised that all those losses would one day be restored, although he didn't guarantee that would happen here on earth. So what's the blessing of persecution? It comes from identifying yourself with Christ. If you endure persecution, it shows that you believe in him enough and trust him enough that you are willing to take whatever comes rather than walk away from him. In the big picture, nothing matters more than following Christ. Nothing in life is worth more than staying close to him—not family, friends, money, fame, acceptance, or even safety.

P

> *Be very glad—for these trials make you partners with Christ in his suffering, so that you will have the wonderful joy of seeing his glory when it is revealed to all the world.*
>
> *—1 Peter 4:13*

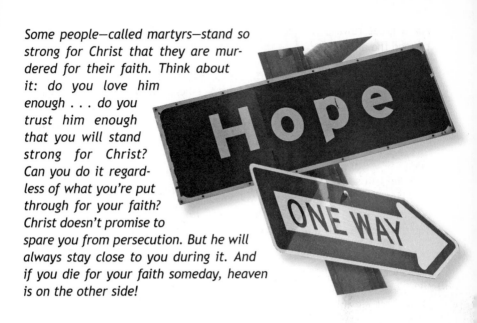

Some people—called martyrs—stand so strong for Christ that they are murdered for their faith. Think about it: do you love him enough . . . do you trust him enough that you will stand strong for Christ? Can you do it regardless of what you're put through for your faith? Christ doesn't promise to spare you from persecution. But he will always stay close to you during it. And if you die for your faith someday, heaven is on the other side!

Possessions

Stuff. We all like stuff. In fact, some people think that the more they have, the more successful they are. People spend a lot of time, energy, and money just trying to get more and more stuff. And once we get it, we hang on tightly to it and keep our stuff locked up. We go to great lengths to stop anyone from taking our stuff. We spend a lot of time taking care of our stuff. But is this obsession with stuff pleasing to God?

P

Possessions

Worry or Trust?
Matthew 6:19-21, 24-33

"Don't store up treasures here on earth, where moths eat them and rust destroys them, and where thieves break in and steal. Store your treasures in heaven, where moths and rust cannot destroy, and thieves do not break in and steal. Wherever your treasure is, there the desires of your heart will also be. . . .

"No one can serve two masters. For you will hate one and love the other; you will be devoted to one and despise the other. You cannot serve both God and money.

> *Share your food with the hungry, and give shelter to the homeless. Give clothes to those who need them, and do not hide from relatives who need your help.*
>
> *—Isaiah 58:7*

"That is why I tell you not to worry about everyday life—whether you have enough food and drink, or enough clothes to wear. Isn't life more than food, and your body more than clothing? Look at the birds. They don't plant or harvest or store food in barns, for your heavenly Father feeds them. And aren't you far more valuable to him than they are? Can all your worries add a single moment to your life?

"And why worry about your clothing? Look at the lilies of the field and how they grow. They don't work or make their clothing, yet Solomon in all his glory was not dressed as beautifully as they are. And if God cares so wonderfully for wildflowers that are here today and thrown into the fire tomorrow, he will certainly care for you. Why do you have so little faith?

"So don't worry about these things, saying, 'What will we eat? What will we drink? What will we wear?' These things dominate the thoughts of unbelievers, but your heavenly Father already knows all your needs. Seek the Kingdom of God above all else, and live righteously, and he will give you everything you need."

P

FOR SALE
BY OWNER

Sharing What You Have
John 6:1-15

Jesus crossed over to the far side of the Sea of Galilee, also known as the Sea of Tiberias. A huge crowd kept following him wherever he went, because they saw his miraculous signs as he healed the sick. Then Jesus climbed a hill and sat down with his disciples around him. (It was nearly time for the Jewish Passover celebration.) Jesus soon saw a huge crowd of people coming to look for him. Turning

to Philip, he asked, "Where can we buy bread to feed all these people?" He was testing Philip, for he already knew what he was going to do.

Philip replied, "Even if we worked for months, we wouldn't have enough money to feed them!"

Then Andrew, Simon Peter's brother, spoke up. "There's a young boy here with five barley loaves and two fish. But what good is that with this huge crowd?"

"Tell everyone to sit down," Jesus said. So they all sat down on the grassy slopes. (The men alone numbered about 5,000.) Then Jesus took the loaves,

> *If someone has enough money to live well and sees a brother or sister in need but shows no compassion— how can God's love be in that person?*
>
> —*1 John 3:17*

gave thanks to God, and distributed them to the people. Afterward he did the same with the fish. And they all ate as much as they wanted. After everyone was full, Jesus told his disciples, "Now gather the leftovers, so that nothing is wasted." So they picked up the pieces and filled twelve baskets with scraps left by the people who had eaten from the five barley loaves.

When the people saw him do this miraculous sign, they exclaimed, "Surely, he is the Prophet we have been expecting!" When Jesus saw that they were ready to force him to be their king, he slipped away into the hills by himself.

Stuff, Stuff, and More Stuff
Luke 12:13-21

Someone called from the crowd, "Teacher, please tell my brother to divide our father's estate with me."

Jesus replied, "Friend, who made me a judge over you to decide such things as that?" Then he said, "Beware! Guard against every kind of greed. Life is not measured by how much you own."

Then he told them a story: "A rich man had a fertile farm that produced fine crops. He said to himself, 'What should I do? I don't have room for all my crops.' Then he said, 'I know! I'll tear down my barns and build bigger ones. Then I'll have room enough to store all my wheat and other goods. And I'll sit back and say to myself, "My friend, you have enough stored away for years to come. Now take it easy! Eat, drink, and be merry!"'

"But God said to him, 'You fool! You will die this very night. Then who will get everything you worked for?'

"Yes, a person is a fool to store up earthly wealth but not have a rich relationship with God."

Okay, are you tracking here? Your relationship with God is way more important than anything you own. If you believe that and live like that, how will your life look?

Well, you'll probably give away your stuff to those who don't have the basics they need to live. You'll spend your time and money helping others instead of being consumed with getting more stuff or playing with your stuff or taking care of your stuff. In other words, the most important thing in your life will be loving God and loving others—not what money can buy!

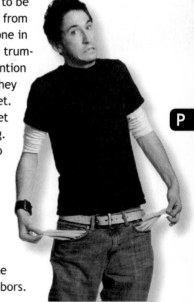

Life isn't fair. Anyone who says it is must be lying or crazy. Life especially isn't fair in the area of money. Some people in this world have more money than they could ever spend—they have everything they want and more. In fact, they don't just have everything—they have the best of everything, and maybe they didn't even work hard to earn it. Then there are people who seem to hit one bad break after the other and can barely make ends meet. Do people who have a lot have a responsibility to the poor of the world? Do those who have anything at all have a responsibility?

Do Not Give to Get
Matthew 6:1-4

"Watch out! Don't do your good deeds publicly, to be admired by others, for you will lose the reward from your Father in heaven. When you give to someone in need, don't do as the hypocrites do—blowing trumpets in the synagogues and streets to call attention to their acts of charity! I tell you the truth, they have received all the reward they will ever get. But when you give to someone in need, don't let your left hand know what your right hand is doing. Give your gifts in private, and your Father, who sees everything, will reward you."

Honor the Poor
Luke 14:12-14

[Jesus] turned to his host. "When you put on a luncheon or a banquet," he said, "don't invite your friends, brothers, relatives, and rich neighbors.

P

109

Poverty

For they will invite you back, and that will be your only reward. Instead, invite the poor, the crippled, the lame, and the blind. Then at the resurrection of the righteous, God will reward you for inviting those who could not repay you."

Give Generously
Mark 10:20-25

"Teacher," the man replied, "I've obeyed all these commandments since I was young."

Looking at the man, Jesus felt genuine love for him. "There is still one thing you haven't done," he told him. "Go and sell all your possessions and give the money to the poor, and you will have treasure in heaven. Then come, follow me."

At this the man's face fell, and he went away sad, for he had many possessions.

Jesus looked around and said to his disciples, "How hard it is for the rich to enter the Kingdom of God!" This amazed them. But Jesus said again, "Dear children, it is very hard to enter the Kingdom of God. In fact, it is easier for a camel to go through the eye of a needle than for a rich person to enter the Kingdom of God!"

Sometimes it is frustrating that wealth is not more evenly shared—at least it's frustrating if you are one of the people without much. Maybe at some point in your life you've felt like other people had a lot more money than you. But did you know that more than half the people in the world live on just a couple of dollars a day? There are people who don't have enough money to know if they will have food tomorrow. Some people do not have homes, money to go to the doctor when they are sick, clothes to wear, or toys to play with.

> **Blessed are those who are generous, because they feed the poor.**
>
> **—Proverbs 22:9**

110

Now think about other people (maybe this is you) who have everything they need—and many things they want. Do these people have a responsibility to the rest of the world? Yep, a big part of being a Christ follower is caring for other people, and that means helping them with physical things like food and clothing. Their spiritual needs are important too, but people are much more likely to listen to what you have to say about God if you've shown you care about their empty stomachs first.

> *Feed the hungry, and help those in trouble. Then your light will shine out from the darkness, and the darkness around you will be as bright as noon.*
>
> *—Isaiah 58:10*

The Bible teaches us to share what we have and help those who have less. That is not just for superrich people—it's for everyone. Help in any way you can, small or big. But when you do, don't forget what Jesus said about your motive: don't do it to get noticed or praised for your generosity. Help someone else anonymously if you can—don't do it so others will pat you on the back and tell you how wonderful you are. Give . . . share . . . help . . . because it's Jesus' command and because you love others.

The Power of God

Have you ever dreamed of having power . . . lots and lots of power? If you have power, you'll be respected and in charge and no one will mess with you, right? Well, let's just say that no one smart will mess with the guy who has the most power—the one *who has power over everything. And who is that, exactly? One thing's for sure: it's not you!*

All Things Are Possible
Mark 10:23-27

Jesus looked around and said to his disciples, "How hard it is for the rich to enter the Kingdom of God!" This amazed them. But Jesus said again, "Dear children, it is very hard to enter the Kingdom of God. In fact, it is easier for a camel to go through the eye of a needle than for a rich person to enter the Kingdom of God!"

The disciples were astounded. "Then who in the world can be saved?" they asked.

Jesus looked at them intently and said, "Humanly speaking, it is impossible. But not with God. Everything is possible with God."

Jesus Has God's Power
Mark 14:60-62

The high priest stood up before the others and asked Jesus, "Well, aren't you going to answer these charges? What do you have to say for yourself?" But Jesus was silent and made no reply. Then the high priest asked him, "Are you the Messiah, the Son of the Blessed One?"

Jesus said, "I AM. And you will see the Son of Man seated in the place of power at God's right hand and coming on the clouds of heaven."

More Powerful Than Anyone Else
John 10:24-30

The people surrounded [Jesus] and asked, "How long are you going to keep us in suspense? If you are the Messiah, tell us plainly."

> *The voice of the LORD echoes above the sea. The God of glory thunders. The LORD thunders over the mighty sea. The voice of the LORD is powerful; the voice of the LORD is majestic.*
>
> *—Psalm 29:3-4*

Jesus replied, "I have already told you, and you don't believe me. The proof is the work I do in my Father's name. But you don't believe me because you are not my sheep. My sheep listen to my voice; I know them, and they follow me. I give them eternal life, and they will never perish. No one can snatch them away from me, for my Father has given them to me, and he is more powerful than anyone else. No one can snatch them from the Father's hand. The Father and I are one."

God's power is amazing, incredible, beyond imagination. It cannot be matched by anyone else or anything else on this earth. It is only God's power that makes it possible for people to enter heaven. It is God's power that forgives sin. It is God's power that is responsible for everything in creation, from the tiniest atom to the tallest mountain, from each individual drop of water to the most gigantic waterfall.

Jesus was both human and God when he came to earth. He taught, did miracles, showed us how to live as God followers, and died and rose again. Then when he went back to heaven, he

P

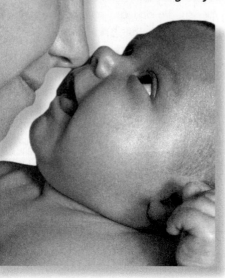

took his place at the right hand of God—meaning all the power of God is in Jesus.

Another amazing thing about God's power is the way it protects his children. Nothing can pull you away from him. As long as you seek him and follow him, he will protect you from anything Satan throws your way, especially the sneak attacks that Satan is so good at. God is more powerful than Satan, more powerful than evil, more powerful than the things that happen in your life. Think about this world spinning in space; think about oceans and mountains and killer whales and hummingbirds; think about a tiny baby whose body has everything it needs to grow and become an adult—you can see that God's power is endless, amazing, and greater than any other power. And his power is working for you—protecting you, guiding you, and empowering you to be the person he wants you to be!

You are worthy, O Lord our God, to receive glory and honor and power. For you created all things, and they exist because you created what you pleased.

—Revelation 4:11

P

Prayer

If you wanted to get to know someone better, you'd probably make an effort to talk to him or her, right? Talking is how we get to know each other and find out what people like and dislike. When you're having problems, you may have a friend you can talk with about it. Talking is key to any relationship. *The same is true of your relationship with God—prayer is just talking to God and listening to him. It's an amazing privilege to be able to have a conversation with the Creator of the universe!*

Honest Prayer
Matthew 6:5-13

"When you pray, don't be like the hypocrites who love to pray publicly on street corners and in the synagogues where everyone can see them. I tell you the truth, that is all the reward they will ever get. But when you pray, go away by yourself, shut the door behind you, and pray to your Father in private. Then your Father, who sees everything, will reward you.

"When you pray, don't babble on and on as people of other religions do. They think their prayers are answered merely by repeating their words again and again. Don't be like them, for your Father knows exactly what you need even before you ask him! Pray like this:

Our Father in heaven, may your name be kept holy.
May your Kingdom come soon.
May your will be done on earth, as it is in heaven.
Give us today the food we need, and forgive us our sins,
as we have forgiven those who sin against us.
And don't let us yield to temptation, but rescue us from the evil one."

P

Be Persistent
Luke 18:1-8

One day Jesus told his disciples a story to show that they should always pray and never give up. "There was a judge in a certain city," he said, "who neither feared God nor cared about people. A widow of that city came to him repeatedly, saying, 'Give me justice in this dispute with my enemy.' The judge ignored her for a while, but finally he said to himself, 'I don't fear God or care about

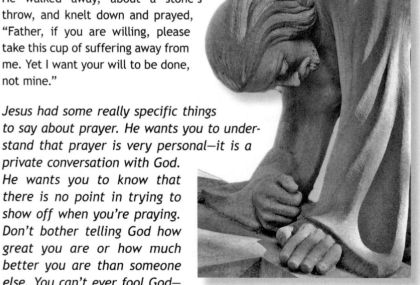

people, but this woman is driving me crazy. I'm going to see that she gets justice, because she is wearing me out with her constant requests!"

Then the Lord said, "Learn a lesson from this unjust judge. Even he rendered a just decision in the end. So don't you think God will surely give justice to his chosen people who cry out to him day and night? Will he keep putting them off? I tell you, he will grant justice to them quickly! But when the Son of Man returns, how many will he find on the earth who have faith?"

Jesus' Prayer
Luke 22:39-42

Accompanied by the disciples, Jesus left the upstairs room and went as usual to the Mount of Olives. There he told them, "Pray that you will not give in to temptation."

He walked away, about a stone's throw, and knelt down and prayed, "Father, if you are willing, please take this cup of suffering away from me. Yet I want your will to be done, not mine."

Jesus had some really specific things to say about prayer. He wants you to understand that prayer is very personal—it is a private conversation with God. He wants you to know that there is no point in trying to show off when you're praying. Don't bother telling God how great you are or how much better you are than someone else. You can't ever fool God— he's not convinced by that kind

P

116

> *If my people who are called by my name will humble themselves and pray and seek my face and turn from their wicked ways, I will hear from heaven and will forgive their sins and restore their land.*
>
> *—2 Chronicles 7:14*

of bragging. God looks at the inside, and he even hears the prayers that are whispered from your heart. Those are often the most honest ones. Don't pray with fancy words so that others who hear you pray will be impressed. That's just showing off.

Jesus encouraged his followers to be persistent in prayer—so bring your requests to God often. That's not because you have to beg God to hear your prayers—it's more because it shows you what things mean enough to you that you pray often about them. In case you've ever wondered if prayer is really that important, remember that Jesus prayed too. It's true that Jesus is God, but when he was on earth, he prayed often. Sometimes he left the crowds behind and went off by himself to connect with God. Sometimes, as he did in the garden of Gethsemane, he asked others to join him in prayer. Jesus even gave us an example of how to pray. It's called the Lord's Prayer (see page 115), and it teaches us to honor God, confess our sins, seek forgiveness and forgive others, and ask for the necessities of life and God's protection. Isn't it amazing that you can talk to God? You can tell him what's important to you and then be still and listen to him speak back to your heart. Don't pass up the opportunity.

> *We are confident that he hears us whenever we ask for anything that pleases him. And since we know he hears us when we make our requests, we also know that he will give us what we ask for.*
>
> *—1 John 5:14-15*

P

Prophecy

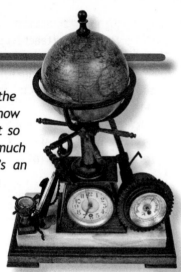

Have you ever wished you could see into the future? Sometimes it would be fun to know what's coming, right? Other times . . . not so much. You may not hear people talking much about prophecy in everyday life, but it's an important part of the Bible. People who lived hundreds of years before Jesus came to earth wrote about his coming and about what would happen to him—that's prophecy. And there are some prophecies in the Bible that are still to come true. . . .

A Prophecy about a Messenger
Matthew 11:7-10

As John's disciples were leaving, Jesus began talking about him to the crowds. "What kind of man did you go into the wilderness to see? Was he a weak reed, swayed by every breath of wind? Or were you expecting to see a man dressed in expensive clothes? No, people with expensive clothes live in palaces. Were you looking for a prophet? Yes, and he is more than a prophet. John is the man to whom the Scriptures refer when they say,

> 'Look, I am sending my messenger ahead of you, and he will prepare your way before you.'"

P

A Prophecy about Jesus' Resurrection
Matthew 20:17-19

As Jesus was going up to Jerusalem, he took the twelve disciples aside privately and told them what was going to happen to him. "Listen," he said, "we're going up to Jerusalem, where the Son of Man will be betrayed to the leading priests and the teachers of religious law. They will sentence him to die. Then they will hand him over to the Romans to be mocked, flogged with a whip, and crucified. But on the third day he will be raised from the dead."

> *Look! I am creating new heavens and a new earth, and no one will even think about the old ones anymore.*
>
> *—Isaiah 65:17*

A Fulfilled Prophecy
Luke 4:17-21

The scroll of Isaiah the prophet was handed to him. He unrolled the scroll and found the place where this was written:

> "The Spirit of the LORD is upon me,
>   for he has anointed me to bring Good News to the poor.
> He has sent me to proclaim that captives will be
>   released,
>   that the blind will see,
>   that the oppressed will be set free,
>   and that the time of the LORD's
>   favor has come."

He rolled up the scroll, handed it back to the attendant, and sat down. All eyes in the synagogue looked at him intently. Then he began to speak to them. "The Scripture you've just heard has been fulfilled this very day!"

Why are the prophecies about Jesus so important? Because the fact that Jesus fulfilled those prophecies one by one, even from the moment of his birth, proved that he is really the Messiah the prophets had written about long ago. Jesus knew who he was, and he announced it to those in the Temple that day. It was up to them to accept that truth. Every other detail in his ministry fulfilled prophecy too.

The people who wrote those early predictions about the Messiah and his life got all that info from God! They wrote down what God told them about the future, including the part about John the Baptist announcing Jesus' ministry before it even began. When Jesus was arrested

P

Protection

> *We are looking forward to the new heavens and new earth he has promised, a world filled with God's righteousness.*
>
> *—2 Peter 3:13*

and executed, his followers could have looked ahead to the future by reading the prophecies written about the Messiah and paying attention to the prophecies Jesus made about himself. Then they would have known that Jesus' work wasn't over, because he would be brought back to life by God's power. God's plan wasn't finished yet!

If you're wondering about the future now, you can read more prophecies given in the Bible about how Jesus will return for his followers and how he is preparing a place for his followers in heaven. The prophecies about Jesus and the prophecies about eternity are a gift from God. We don't have to wonder what's going to happen . . . we just need to prepare for it!

Protection

How would you like to have a bodyguard walk around with you all the time—someone who could protect you from bullies and run interference for you in crowds and make sure you always get to the front of lines? You would always feel safe and protected. Well, unless you are rich and famous, that probably isn't going to happen. So where does your protection come from?

Don't Be Afraid
Matthew 10:26-31

"Don't be afraid of those who threaten you. For the time is coming when everything that is covered will be revealed, and all that is secret will be made known to all. What I tell you now in the darkness, shout abroad when daybreak comes. What I whisper in your ear, shout from the housetops for all to hear!

"Don't be afraid of those who want to kill your body; they cannot touch your soul. Fear only God, who can destroy both soul and body in hell. What is the price of two sparrows—one copper coin? But not a single sparrow can fall to the ground without your Father knowing it. And the very hairs on your head are all numbered. So don't be afraid; you are more valuable to God than a whole flock of sparrows."

Constant Protection
John 17:1-5, 9-12

Jesus looked up to heaven and said, "Father, the hour has come. Glorify your Son so he can give glory back to you. For you have given him authority over everyone. He gives eternal life to each one you have given him. And this is the way to have eternal life—to know you, the only true God, and Jesus Christ, the one you sent to earth. I brought glory to you here on earth by completing the work you gave me to do. Now, Father, bring me into the glory we shared before the world began. . . .

"My prayer is not for the world, but for those you have given me, because they belong to you. All who are mine belong to you, and you have given them to me, so they bring me glory. Now I am departing from the world; they are staying in this world, but I am coming to you. Holy Father, you have given me your name; now protect them by the power of your name so that they will be united just as we are. During my time here, I protected them by the power of the name you gave me. I guarded them so that not one was lost, except the one headed for destruction, as the Scriptures foretold."

> *The LORD is a shelter for the oppressed, a refuge in times of trouble.*
>
> *—Psalm 9:9*

P

If you've spent any chunk of time on this planet, chances are you have felt unprotected

Protection

at some point . . . like life is caving in around you. Maybe there's a kid who seems to get great joy from picking on you, either by smacking you around or making fun of you in front of others. Maybe you want protection from pain or bad health that keeps pushing you down. It could be that you need protection from a mean or critical adult in your life. Or—the sneakiest of all problems—you need serious protection from the temptations and attacks that Satan dumps on you. But here's the good news: you have protection that is stronger than any armor a soldier ever wore. Your protector is more powerful than any army that ever existed. Your protector pays personal attention to you and what's going on in your life. He knows every danger you face, big and small, and all the attacks that will come on your faith.

God is on duty constantly, 24-7, watching over you and watching out for you. What's your responsibility? To grab on to that protection and hang on tight. Stay close to God. He will help you guard your heart—that's where temptation, discouragement, and sin begin. All the protection you could need or want is available to you. Just stay close to God by reading his Word and talking with him daily. Ask for his help in guarding your heart against all Satan's attacks. God will protect you!

> **The Lord is faithful; he will strengthen you and guard you from the evil one.**
>
> **—2 Thessalonians 3:3**

P

Purpose

How many zillion times have you been asked, "What do you want to be when you grow up?" That question gets old after a while, especially if you feel some pressure to answer a certain way. But do you sometimes ask yourself why you are on this planet? Do you ever wonder what it is God wants you to do with your life? What you're looking for is . . . purpose.

Salt and Light
Matthew 5:13-16

"You are the salt of the earth. But what good is salt if it has lost its flavor? Can you make it salty again? It will be thrown out and trampled underfoot as worthless.

"You are the light of the world—like a city on a hilltop that cannot be hidden. No one lights a lamp and then puts it under a basket. Instead, a lamp is placed on a stand, where it gives

P

Purpose

light to everyone in the house. In the same way, let your good deeds shine out for all to see, so that everyone will praise your heavenly Father."

What's Most Important?
Matthew 16:24-28

Jesus said to his disciples, "If any of you wants to be my follower, you must turn from your selfish ways, take up your cross, and follow me. If you try to hang on to your life, you will lose it. But if you give up your life for my sake, you will save it. And what do you benefit if you gain the whole world but lose your own soul? Is anything worth more than your soul? For the Son of Man will come with his angels in the glory of his Father and will judge all people according to their deeds. And I tell you the truth, some standing here right now will not die before they see the Son of Man coming in his Kingdom."

Walk in the Light
John 8:12

Jesus spoke to the people once more and said, "I am the light of the world. If you follow me, you won't have to walk in darkness, because you will have the light that leads to life."

God did not plop you down on this planet to be a paperweight. He has a particular job for you that will contribute to his work, the world, and the people around you. You have purpose and value, and no one else could take your place. Granted, that may be difficult to believe when you are surrounded by people who seem super talented or who do things you think you could never do. Some people seem to have such amazing opportunities . . . and you just feel ordinary. If you focus on these kinds of thoughts, you

> *"I know the plans I have for you," says the LORD. "They are plans for good and not for disaster, to give you a future and a hope."*
>
> *—Jeremiah 29:11*

124

> *Lead a life worthy of your calling, for you have been called by God.*
>
> *—Ephesians 4:1*

quickly begin feeling like you are on God's B team and like your accomplishments are second rate. But that isn't true—you have a specific purpose in God's plan, something he wants you to do. Jesus had a purpose when he came to earth too. He knew what his job was, and he stayed focused on doing it.

God gives each of his children the ability to do certain things well. Some of those are more "up front" kinds of abilities, such as singing or speaking or leading. Some abilities are more behind the scenes, like being a good listener or serving or organizing. Remember that God's purposes for you will usually involve your abilities and things you love . . . because he's the one who planted those things in you in the first place. So pay attention to what you enjoy and to the opportunities that come your way. Then thank God for the purposes he has for you on this earth!

> *Understand this, my dear brothers and sisters: You must all be quick to listen, slow to speak, and slow to get angry.*
>
> *—James 1:19*

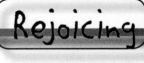

Rejoicing

Your team wins the championship. You get an A on an extra-tough test. You get to celebrate your birthday with all your best friends. What other kinds of things make you jump in the air with cheers blasting from your mouth? Some things just make you happy to be in your skin . . . some things make you rejoice. Did you know that God rejoices too?

R

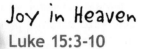

Joy in Heaven
Luke 15:3-10

Jesus told them this story: "If a man has a hundred sheep and one of them gets lost, what will he do? Won't he leave the ninety-nine others in the wilderness and go to search for the one that is lost until he finds it? And when he has found it, he will joyfully carry it home on his shoulders. When he arrives, he will call together his friends and neighbors, saying, 'Rejoice with me because I have found my lost sheep.' In the same way, there is more joy in heaven over one lost sinner who repents and returns to God than over ninety-nine others who are righteous and haven't strayed away!

"Or suppose a woman has ten silver coins and loses one. Won't she light a lamp and sweep the entire house and search carefully until she finds it? And when she finds it, she will call in her friends and neighbors and say, 'Rejoice with me because I have found my lost coin.' In the same way, there is joy in the presence of God's angels when even one sinner repents."

> *The LORD your God is living among you. He is a mighty savior. He will take delight in you with gladness. With his love, he will calm all your fears. He will rejoice over you with joyful songs.*
> —*Zephaniah 3:17*

The Lost Son
Luke 15:11-13, 20, 23-24

R

Jesus told them this story: "A man had two sons. The younger son told his father, 'I want my share of your estate now before you die.' So his father agreed to divide his wealth between his sons.

"A few days later this younger son packed all his belongings and moved to a distant land, and there he wasted all his money in wild living. . . .

> *Always be full of joy in the Lord. I say it again— rejoice!*
> —*Philippians 4:4*

126

He returned home to his father. And while he was still a long way off, his father saw him coming. Filled with love and compassion, he ran to his son, embraced him, and kissed him. . . . "We must celebrate with a feast, for this son of mine was dead and has now returned to life. He was lost, but now he is found." So the party began.

Doesn't happy-out-of-your-skin celebrating feel sooooo good? Rejoicing is energizing and stress relieving, and it's an important part of life. There are many things to celebrate—from forgiveness to birthdays to good friends to championships to actual miracles. Even when things are pretty stinky, if you look around you can probably find something to rejoice about. Jesus encourages his followers to celebrate their lives, because life is a gift from God. We can rejoice in the very fact that we have life.

The major reason to rejoice, though, is God himself. Can you believe that the God of the universe—the creator of everything there is, the ultimate judge of all people—cares about you? He is concerned about even the smallest details of your life. The thing he cares about most is when people come to know him. When you lose something valuable and then find it, don't you dance around with joy? That's how God feels when a lost soul comes to him! In the story of the lost son, the father has agonized over his lost son, so when the boy comes home, the dad throws a party of all parties. That's real rejoicing! The Bible says that is what happens in heaven when you accept Christ as your Savior. Happy, happy times!

R

Repentance

When you do something wrong, what is your typical reaction? Do you tend to make excuses or get defensive? Do you put the blame on someone else? Repentance means admitting when you're wrong and saying you're sorry . . . and meaning it! Yeah, that last part is really important: you have to mean it, otherwise you're just putting on a good show for others. Some people think it makes them look good to act like they are sorry even if they aren't. The thing is, they don't fool God.

The Kingdom Is Near
Matthew 4:17

From then on Jesus began to preach, "Repent of your sins and turn to God, for the Kingdom of Heaven is near."

The Way to Forgiveness
Luke 24:44-48

[Jesus] said, "When I was with you before, I told you that everything written about me in the law of Moses and the prophets and in the Psalms must be fulfilled." Then he opened their minds to understand the Scriptures. And he said, "Yes, it was written long ago that the Messiah would suffer and die and rise from the dead on the third day. It was also written that this message would be proclaimed in the authority of his name to all the nations, beginning in Jerusalem: 'There is forgiveness of sins for all who repent.' You are witnesses of all these things."

R

Wake Up!
Revelation 3:1-6

"Write this letter to the angel of the church in Sardis. This is the message from the one who has the seven-fold Spirit of God and the seven stars:

"I know all the things you do, and that you have a reputation for being alive—but you are dead. Wake up! Strengthen what little remains, for even what is left is almost dead. I find that your actions do not meet the requirements of my God. Go back to what you heard and believed at first; hold to it firmly. Repent and turn to me again. If you don't wake up, I will come to you suddenly, as unexpected as a thief.

"Yet there are some in the church in Sardis who have not soiled their clothes with evil. They will walk with me in white, for they are worthy. All who are victorious will be clothed in white. I will never erase their names from the Book of Life, but I will announce before my Father and his angels that they are mine.

"Anyone with ears to hear must listen to the Spirit and understand what he is saying to the churches."

Repentance is not something to take lightly. You might be able to fool people around you by pretending to be sorry for wrong things you've done . . . but you'll never fool God. He can see your heart, so he knows if you are truly sorry or not. Jesus was pretty serious about repentance: it is impossible to be his follower without turning away from your sin. God takes sin very seriously—he can't allow anything unclean into heaven. The only way to get rid of your sin is to confess it and repent of it. Then, because

> *If we claim we have no sin, we are only fooling ourselves and not living in the truth. But if we confess our sins to him, he is faithful and just to forgive us our sins and to cleanse us from all wickedness.*
>
> *—1 John 1:8-9*

R

Resurrection

of Jesus' death and resurrection, that sin is washed away and completely forgotten. God went to great lengths so we don't have to stay in our sin!

Some people think they can take their time getting to repentance. They think they can live their lives any way they want and have all kinds of "fun" and not deal with the problem of their sin until someday when they're older. Jesus made it clear that is not a good idea. He said that God's Kingdom is near. No one knows when Jesus is going to return to take his followers to heaven to be with him. For that matter, no one knows when his or her life on this earth is going to end. So don't put off repentance for any reason. Turn away from your sins, and live your life for Jesus. Take note of Jesus' warning to the church in Revelation 3:1-6, and make sure you are living your life to serve and honor him. The first step to making your life count for God is to repent!

> *You do not desire a sacrifice, or I would offer one. You do not want a burnt offering. The sacrifice you desire is a broken spirit. You will not reject a broken and repentant heart, O God.*
> —Psalm 51:16-17

R

Resurrection

Unless it's Easter Sunday, chances are pretty good that you won't hear the word resurrection very often. Most people in our world think death is pretty much the end—once you're in the ground, it's game over. But Christians know that this life is not all there is. Three days after Jesus died, he was raised from the dead, or resurrected. And since he defeated death, it means there's good news for us, too. . . .

As It Was Written
Luke 24:46-48

[Jesus] said, "Yes, it was written long ago that the Messiah would suffer and die and rise from the dead on the third day. It was also written that this message would be proclaimed in the authority of his name to all the nations, beginning in Jerusalem: 'There is forgiveness of sins for all who repent.' You are witnesses of all these things."

The Father Gives Life
John 5:19-21

Jesus explained, "I tell you the truth, the Son can do nothing by himself. He does only what he sees the Father doing. Whatever the Father does, the Son also does. For the Father loves the Son and shows him everything he is doing. In fact, the Father will show him how to do even greater works than healing this man. Then you will truly be astonished. For just as the Father gives life to those he raises from the dead, so the Son gives life to anyone he wants."

The Dead Will Rise
John 5:25-29

"I assure you that the time is coming, indeed it's here now, when the dead will hear my voice—the voice of the Son of God. And those who listen will live. The Father has life in himself, and he has granted that

R

Resurrection

> *When our dying bodies have been transformed into bodies that will never die, this Scripture will be fulfilled: "Death is swallowed up in victory."*
>
> *—1 Corinthians 15:54*

same life-giving power to his Son. And he has given him authority to judge everyone because he is the Son of Man. Don't be so surprised! Indeed, the time is coming when all the dead in their graves will hear the voice of God's Son, and they will rise again. Those who have done good will rise to experience eternal life, and those who have continued in evil will rise to experience judgment."

God raised Jesus back to life after he was murdered. That

is the resurrection. Then Jesus went back to heaven to be with God. But before Jesus left earth, he made it clear that someday he will return for the single purpose of taking his followers back to heaven with him. The Bible says that all the Christ followers who have died will be raised back to life. This promise shows that God has complete power over death. That means that death doesn't have the final say for you, either. In Christ, you will experience resurrection too! In other words, dead is not forever. It still hurts when you lose family members or friends to death, but if those loved

R

> *I want to know Christ and experience the mighty power that raised him from the dead. I want to suffer with him, sharing in his death, so that one way or another I will experience the resurrection from the dead!*
>
> *—Philippians 3:10-11*

ones knew Christ, they will live forever in eternity with him. So you will see the people you've had to say good-bye to again! How cool is that?

God proved he is strong enough and powerful enough to conquer death when he raised Jesus back to life. Then he promised that his followers would have the same victory over death. Resurrection is why you can absolutely plan on being in heaven forever. Dead is not forever!

Rewards

A reward is like thick, gooey frosting on your favorite cake. The cake itself is a treat, but to get the frosting, too . . . yum! You might get a reward for winning a big contest or for returning something another person lost. God gives rewards too, but sometimes his rewards come at surprising times or in unexpected ways.

R

Reward for Staying Strong
Matthew 5:11-12

"God blesses you when people mock you and persecute you and lie about you and say all sorts of evil things against you because you are my followers. Be happy about it! Be very glad! For a great reward awaits you in heaven. And remember, the ancient prophets were persecuted in the same way."

> *God blesses those who patiently endure testing and temptation. Afterward they will receive the crown of life that God has promised to those who love him.*
> —James 1:12

Reward for Secret Good Deeds
Matthew 6:1-4

"Watch out! Don't do your good deeds publicly, to be admired by others, for you will lose the reward from your Father in heaven. When you give to someone in need, don't do as the hypocrites do—blowing trumpets in the synagogues and streets to call attention to their acts of charity! I tell you the truth, they have received all the reward they will ever get. But when you give to someone in need, don't let your left hand know what your right hand is doing. Give your gifts in private, and your Father, who sees everything, will reward you."

Reward Is Coming
Mark 10:29-31

"I assure you that everyone who has given up house or brothers or sisters or mother or father or children or property, for my sake and for the Good News, will receive now in return a hundred times as many houses, brothers, sisters, mothers, children, and property—along with persecution. And in the world to come that person will have eternal life. But many who are the greatest now will be least important then, and those who seem least important now will be the greatest then."

Jesus promised amazing rewards to his followers. What do you have to do to get these rewards? Well, it's not always going to be simple. Sometimes people will pick on you just because you try to live for God. And it may not just be cruel words—

> **Physical training is good, but training for godliness is much better, promising benefits in this life and in the life to come.**
>
> **—1 Timothy 4:8**

people may try to physically hurt you too. Jesus said to accept whatever treatment is given to you without giving up. Don't get discouraged, because you know you will have a reward waiting for you in heaven, just as Jesus promised. Jesus mentioned a couple of conditions for receiving the rewards he spoke about. One is that when you help others or do things for other people, you do it humbly. Don't have a "look at me" attitude and try to show off how wonderful you are. If you draw attention to yourself and pat yourself on the back . . . well, that's your reward, so don't expect anything more. The other condition is to put Jesus before anything and anyone else. Choose to obey whatever God asks you to do, even if that means letting go of people or things you love. Don't let anything be more important to you than God. When you serve him with your whole heart, your reward will be waiting for you in heaven.

R

Sacrifice

Do you consider yourself to be a generous person? Perhaps you do because you toss some money in the offering at youth group or church. Maybe you share your lunch or give really nice Christmas gifts. But are you generous to the point of giv-ing sacrificially? Giving until it hurts? Giving until you have nothing left? That, my friend, is sacrifice.

Jesus' Example
Mark 10:42-45

Jesus called them together and said, "You know that the rulers in this world lord it over their people, and officials flaunt their authority over those under them. But among you it will be different. Whoever wants to be a leader among you must be your servant, and whoever wants to be first among you must be the slave of everyone else. For even the Son of Man came not to be served but to serve others and to give his life as a ransom for many."

Give It All Away!
Matthew 19:21

Jesus told him, "If you want to be perfect, go and sell all your possessions and give the money to the poor, and you will have treasure in heaven. Then come, follow me."

S

The Widow's Offering
Mark 12:43-44

Jesus called his disciples to him and said, "I tell you the truth, this poor widow has given more than all the others who are making contributions. For they gave a tiny part of their surplus, but she, poor as she is, has given everything she had to live on."

> *Wherever you go, I will go; wherever you live, I will live. Your people will be my people, and your God will be my God.*
>
> —*Ruth 1:16*

Lay Down Your Life
John 15:12-17

"This is my commandment: Love each other in the same way I have loved you. There is no greater love than to lay down one's life for one's friends. You are my friends if you do what I command. I no longer call you slaves, because a master doesn't confide in his slaves. Now you are my friends, since I have told you everything the Father told me. You didn't choose me. I chose you. I appointed you to go and produce lasting fruit, so that the Father will give you whatever you ask for, using my name. This is my command: Love each other."

There is a socially acceptable level of giving to those in need—and that is

S

Sacrifice

what many people live by. They give the leftovers of their time and money, or they give only when it's convenient. These kinds of givers try to get by with just enough. But Jesus said that isn't good enough. His example of giving is the standard. He left the glory of heaven to come to earth and become a servant to the very people who would one day kill him. That's real sacrifice.

Jesus often taught about giving sacrificially to others—in fact, he told one person to sell everything he had and give the money to the poor! Yeah, that didn't go over so well. When Jesus saw the woman in the Temple put her last two cents in the offering plate, he used her as an example of sacrificial giving and praised her generosity. That woman's heart truly belonged to God, and her gift demonstrated that sacrifice isn't just about money—it's really about love. Jesus said that if you really and truly love someone, you will be willing to lay down your life for that person. Does that mean literally dying? Probably not. More than likely, it will mean giving of your time, your energy, your money, and your stuff as generously as possible . . . until it hurts. In fact, give it all away, if that is what God leads you to do!

> You know that God paid a ransom to save you from the empty life you inherited from your ancestors. And the ransom he paid was not mere gold or silver. It was the precious blood of Christ, the sinless, spotless Lamb of God.
>
> —1 Peter 1:18-19

S

Sadness

Feeling sad stinks, doesn't it? You might think that God would just fix all the sadness so that no one ever has to feel down again. Well, yeah, that would be wonderful, but it isn't going to happen on this earth. This world is broken because people choose to disobey God. And because it is a broken world filled with broken people, sadness is a part of life. In fact, it's something even Jesus experienced.

Jesus Faces Grief
Matthew 26:36-39

Jesus went with [his disciples] to the olive grove called Gethsemane, and he said, "Sit here while I go over there to pray." He took Peter and Zebedee's two sons, James and John, and he became anguished and distressed. He told them, "My soul is crushed with grief to the point of death. Stay here and keep watch with me."

He went on a little farther and bowed with his face to the ground, praying, "My Father! If it is possible, let this cup of suffering be taken away from me. Yet I want your will to be done, not mine."

Jesus Weeps
Luke 19:41-44

As [Jesus] came closer to Jerusalem and saw the city ahead, he began to weep. "How I wish today that you of all people would understand the way to peace.

S

Sadness

But now it is too late, and peace is hidden from your eyes. Before long your enemies will build ramparts against your walls and encircle you and close in on you from every side. They will crush you into the ground, and your children with you. Your enemies will not leave a single stone in place, because you did not accept your opportunity for salvation."

Sadness Turns to Joy
John 16:16-22

"In a little while you won't see me anymore. But a little while after that, you will see me again."

Some of the disciples asked each other, "What does he mean when he says, 'In a little while you won't see me, but then you will see me,' and 'I am going to the Father'? And what does he mean by 'a little while'? We don't understand."

Jesus realized they wanted to ask him about it, so he said, "Are you asking yourselves what I meant? I said in a little while you won't see me, but a little while after that you will see me again. I tell you the truth, you will weep and mourn over what is going to happen to me, but the world will rejoice. You will grieve, but your grief will suddenly turn to wonderful joy. It will be like a woman suffering the pains of labor. When her child is born, her anguish gives way to joy because she has brought a new baby into the world. So you have sorrow now, but I will see you again; then you will rejoice, and no one can rob you of that joy."

> *He will wipe every tear from their eyes, and there will be no more death or sorrow or crying or pain. All these things are gone forever.*
>
> *—Revelation 21:4*

S

Jesus understands what it feels like to be human. He has personally experienced sadness, loneliness, anger, and happiness. He understands all our emotions because he lived for thirty-three years on this earth in a human body. That means he cares and he can help you get through whatever you're facing.

Scripture records in a couple of places that Jesus cried when he was hurting deeply. Once he wept over a city filled with people who just couldn't seem to get who he was—people who refused his message. He also cried when his friend Lazarus died. His prayer in the garden of Gethsemane, when he knew he was going to be arrested and put through some terrible things until he was finally crucified, showed his extreme grief. Yet in his sadness, Jesus never stopped serving God. He never gave up hope that God was in control. He trusted God completely. Jesus knew that his followers would be sad when he died, and it was okay that they were sad. But he reminded them that they could still have hope in their sadness because one day he would return and take them back to heaven.

So remember that it's okay to be sad. Grief shows that you cared a lot about someone or something. But never give up the hope that God will make things right someday. He will, because he loves you and he is working in your life and the lives of those you love. When you're sad, you can tell God about it and trust him to give you hope for the future.

> He was despised and rejected—a man of sorrows, acquainted with deepest grief. We turned our backs on him and looked the other way. He was despised, and we did not care.
>
> —Isaiah 53:3

S

Salvation

When you hear about people being saved, it usually means they were rescued from some terrible disaster. Maybe they were stranded on their roof because of a huge storm and a helicopter came to get them, or maybe they were pulled out of a burning building by a brave firefighter. There is another kind of saving though—and it concerns eternity. Because God loves people so much, he made a plan to rescue us from our sins so we can join him in heaven one day. That is real salvation.

The Gateway to Life
Matthew 7:13-14

"You can enter God's Kingdom only through the narrow gate. The highway to hell is broad, and its gate is wide for the many who choose that way. But the gateway to life is very narrow and the road is difficult, and only a few ever find it."

Don't Fake It
Matthew 7:21-23

"Not everyone who calls out to me, 'Lord! Lord!' will enter the Kingdom of Heaven. Only those who actually do the will of my Father in heaven will enter. On judgment day many will say to me, 'Lord! Lord! We prophesied in your name and cast out demons in your name and performed many miracles in your name.' But I will reply, 'I never knew you. Get away from me, you who break God's laws.'"

Be Born Again
John 3:3, 5-7

Jesus replied, "I tell you the truth, unless you are born again, you cannot see the Kingdom of God. . . . I assure you, no one can enter the Kingdom of God without being born of water and the Spirit. Humans can reproduce only human life, but the Holy Spirit gives birth to spiritual life. So don't be surprised when I say, 'You must be born again.'"

God Made a Way
John 3:16-21

"God loved the world so much that he gave his one and only Son, so that everyone who believes in him will not perish but have eternal life. God sent his Son into the world not to judge the world, but to save the world through him.

"There is no judgment against anyone who believes in him. But anyone who does not believe in him has already been judged for not believing in God's one and only Son. And the judgment is based on this fact: God's light came into the world, but people loved the darkness more than the light, for their actions were evil. All who do evil hate the light and refuse to go near it for fear their sins will be exposed. But those who do what is right come to the light so others can see that they are doing what God wants."

> *Christ died for us so that, whether we are dead or alive when he returns, we can live with him forever.*
>
> *—1 Thessalonians 5:10*

Maybe you think salvation is something you don't have to think about until you're old. Actually, it is a topic of highest importance that needs your consideration right now, regardless of how old you are. There are people in the world who claim that there are lots of ways to get to heaven. They say that a loving God wouldn't be so "exclusive." But

S

Serving God

> *Everyone who calls on the name of the LORD will be saved.*
>
> —Romans 10:13

the truth is, there is only one way to salvation. And God isn't exclusive—he has made salvation available to everyone who will turn to him. The doorway to heaven is narrow because there is only one way to get through it—by confessing your sins and accepting Jesus as your Savior. This is God's special plan—it's the reason he gave his only Son to come to earth, live, teach, die, and be raised back to life.

Why did God come up with this plan for salvation? Why would he sacrifice his only Son? Simple . . . he loves you. The Bible says that God loves the world, and that includes you as an individual. If you were the only person on the planet, would Jesus have come to save you? Yes. God loves you, so he came up with a plan for your salvation. God wants everyone to have the chance to choose salvation and be with him in heaven. If you haven't accepted his plan of salvation, do it today!

Serving God

When people are talking about their dreams for the future, do you ever hear them hoping to be a servant someday? Doesn't sound like a very high aspiration, does it? Especially when other people are striving to be CEOs, famous musicians, or professional athletes. For the most part, the world encourages you to reach higher than servanthood—you should want to be the boss! But in Jesus' plan, servanthood is exactly what you want to strive for. After all, Jesus himself was a servant to the people in his world.

> *You must fear the LORD your God and serve him.*
>
> *—Deuteronomy 6:13*

Who Will You Serve?
Matthew 4:8-10

The devil took [Jesus] to the peak of a very high mountain and showed him all the kingdoms of the world and their glory. "I will give it all to you," he said, "if you will kneel down and worship me."

"Get out of here, Satan," Jesus told him. "For the Scriptures say, 'You must worship the LORD your God and serve only him.'"

Can You Serve Two Masters?
Luke 16:1-13

Jesus told this story to his disciples: "There was a certain rich man who had a manager handling his affairs. One day a report came that the manager was wasting his employer's money. So the employer called him in and said, 'What's this I hear about you? Get your report in order, because you are going to be fired.'

"The manager thought to himself, 'Now what? My boss has fired me. I don't have the strength to dig ditches, and I'm too proud to beg. Ah, I know how to ensure that I'll have plenty of friends who will give me a home when I am fired.'

"So he invited each person who owed money to his employer to come and discuss the situation. He asked the first one, 'How much do you owe him?' The man replied, 'I owe him 800 gallons of olive oil.' So the manager told him, 'Take the bill and quickly change it to 400 gallons.'

Serving God

"'And how much do you owe my employer?' he asked the next man. 'I owe him 1,000 bushels of wheat,' was the reply. 'Here,' the manager said, 'take the bill and change it to 800 bushels.'

"The rich man had to admire the dishonest rascal for being so shrewd. And it is true that the children of this world are more shrewd in dealing with the world around them than are the children of the light. Here's the lesson: Use your worldly resources to benefit others and make friends. Then, when your earthly possessions are gone, they will welcome you to an eternal home.

"If you are faithful in little things, you will be faithful in large ones. But if you are dishonest in little things, you won't be honest with greater responsibilities. And if you are untrustworthy about worldly wealth, who will trust you with the true riches of heaven? And if you are not faithful with other people's things, why should you be trusted with things of your own?

"No one can serve two masters. For you will hate one and love the other; you will be devoted to one and despise the other. You cannot serve both God and money."

> *Be very careful to obey all the commands and the instructions that Moses gave to you. Love the LORD your God, walk in all his ways, obey his commands, hold firmly to him, and serve him with all your heart and all your soul.*
>
> *—Joshua 22:5*

Whether you realize it or not, you are always serving someone or something. Everyone is. Some people think they are completely independent and don't serve anyone or anything. They are wrong. Every person on this planet has a master of some kind, whether it's money or popularity or grades or something else. For some people it's friends. If your friends have the most powerful influence over the choices you make and the things you do, then you are serving your friends. Another thing you could be serving are your interests—if your number one priority is a certain sport or music and you spend your time and energy pursuing that. Get the idea? You do serve something.

Jesus taught that the best choice is to serve God—and that you can't serve more than one master. Meaning God can't be tied with anything else in your life for first place.

It's pretty simple: two people can't be in charge in your life. Some people try to serve God when it's convenient but then serve something else when that's more convenient. That may seem to work for a while, and they might even fool people around them into thinking they are devoted Christ followers. But they're not fooling God. He sees their divided hearts. Eventually they get so tired of this two-master thing that they end up ignoring or hating one of them.

Be careful, because you never want to put yourself in the position of hating God.

The Shepherd

A shepherd is somebody who is in charge. A shepherd is in charge of keeping the sheep safe, making sure they have food and water, and getting the flock from one place to another. It's a big responsibility. Jesus called himself a shepherd too . . . the Good Shepherd.

S

The Shepherd

The Shepherd's Voice
John 10:1-5

"I tell you the truth, anyone who sneaks over the wall of a sheepfold, rather than going through the gate, must surely be a thief and a robber! But the one who enters through the gate is the shepherd of the sheep. The gatekeeper opens the gate for him, and the sheep recognize his voice and come to him. He calls his own sheep by name and leads them out. After he has gathered his own flock, he walks ahead of them, and they follow him because they know his voice. They won't follow a stranger; they will run from him because they don't know his voice."

> *The Lamb on the throne will be their Shepherd. He will lead them to springs of life-giving water. And God will wipe every tear from their eyes.*
> —**Revelation 7:17**

The Good Shepherd
John 10:11-16

"I am the good shepherd. The good shepherd sacrifices his life for the sheep. A hired hand will run when he sees a wolf coming. He will abandon the sheep because they don't belong to him and he isn't their shepherd. And so the wolf attacks them and scatters the flock. The hired hand runs away because he's working only for the money and doesn't really care about the sheep.

"I am the good shepherd; I know my own sheep, and they know me, just as my Father knows me and I know the Father. So I sacrifice my life for the sheep. I have other sheep, too, that are not in this sheepfold. I must bring them

S

148

also. They will listen to my voice, and there will be one flock with one shepherd."

Feed My Sheep

John 21:15-17

After breakfast Jesus asked Simon Peter, "Simon son of John, do you love me more than these?"

"Yes, Lord," Peter replied, "you know I love you."

"Then feed my lambs," Jesus told him.

> *May the God of peace— who brought up from the dead our Lord Jesus, the great Shepherd of the sheep, and ratified an eternal covenant with his blood—may he equip you with all you need for doing his will. May he produce in you, through the power of Jesus Christ, every good thing that is pleasing to him. All glory to him forever and ever! Amen.*
>
> *—Hebrews 13:20-21*

Jesus repeated the question: "Simon son of John, do you love me?"

"Yes, Lord," Peter said, "you know I love you."

"Then take care of my sheep," Jesus said.

A third time he asked him, "Simon son of John, do you love me?"

Peter was hurt that Jesus asked the question a third time. He said, "Lord, you know everything. You know that I love you."

Jesus said, "Then feed my sheep."

Being a shepherd is not an easy job, because sometimes the sheep decide they don't want to follow their shepherd. Sometimes a sheep will wander off by itself and do its own thing. That always means trouble or danger. Some sheep decide to follow someone who is not their shepherd, and that's a problem too. When Jesus told stories about sheep, he was really talking about people. Jesus called himself the Good Shepherd, and he cares a lot about his flock. He wants his people to follow him so he can protect us from Satan, who is always trying to steal sheep from Jesus' flock. The Good Shepherd knows every sheep that belongs to him, and he knows when Satan is going after one of them.

S

Sin

If you are really a part of Jesus' flock, then you will know Jesus' voice. You will know when Jesus is telling you to do something or go this way or that. You will know when the voice that's telling you to do something is actually Satan. Jesus will protect you. The Good Shepherd provides food and water for his flock—the Word of God is the food, and the refreshment of pray-

ing and worshiping is the water. Jesus gives his flock everything we need if we will follow his voice. Jesus also gave his followers jobs to help take care of the rest of his flock. He told Peter to feed his sheep. You have a job to do too—something God has called you specifically to do. The Good Shepherd wants you to help take care of his flock. What can you do to help feed his sheep?

Sin isn't really a popular topic in casual conversation. Most people would prefer not to think about it . . . or they assume that sin is only the really big stuff, like murder. But according to Jesus, sin is unkind words. Sin is selfishness. Sin is cheating. Sin is greed. Sin is disobeying God's laws and commands. Sin is all the evil things people do or think or say. Ever since Adam and Eve first disobeyed God in the Garden of Eden, sin comes naturally to us. Sin is not allowed in heaven. That means we would all be excluded. But there is one way to escape sin. . . .

S

A Slave of Sin
John 8:31-38

Jesus said to the people who believed in him, "You are truly my disciples if you remain faithful to my teachings. And you will know the truth, and the truth will set you free."

"But we are descendants of Abraham," they said. "We have never been slaves to anyone. What do you mean, 'You will be set free'?"

Jesus replied, "I tell you the truth, everyone who sins is a slave of sin. A slave is not a permanent member of the family, but a son is part of the family forever. So if the Son sets you free, you are truly free. Yes, I realize that you are descendants of Abraham. And yet some of you are trying to kill me because there's no room in your hearts for my message. I am telling you what I saw when I was with my Father. But you are following the advice of your father."

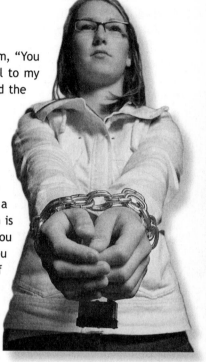

The One Sin That Can't Be Forgiven
Matthew 12:30-37

> *Everyone has sinned; we all fall short of God's glorious standard.*
>
> —*Romans 3:23*

"Anyone who isn't with me opposes me, and anyone who isn't working with me is actually working against me.

"So I tell you, every sin and blasphemy can be forgiven—except blasphemy against the Holy Spirit, which will never be forgiven. Anyone who speaks against the Son of Man can be forgiven, but anyone who speaks against the Holy Spirit will never be forgiven, either in this world or in the world to come.

S

Sin

> *Temptation comes from our own desires, which entice us and drag us away. These desires give birth to sinful actions. And when sin is allowed to grow, it gives birth to death.*
>
> —James 1:14-15

"A tree is identified by its fruit. If a tree is good, its fruit will be good. If a tree is bad, its fruit will be bad. You brood of snakes! How could evil men like you speak what is good and right? For whatever is in your heart determines what you say. A good person produces good things from the treasury of a good heart, and an evil person produces evil things from the treasury of an evil heart. And I tell you this, you must give an account on judgment day for every idle word you speak. The words you say will either acquit you or condemn you."

Unless You Believe . . .

John 8:21-24

Jesus said to them again, "I am going away. You will search for me but will die in your sin. You cannot come where I am going."

The people asked, "Is he planning to commit suicide? What does he mean, 'You cannot come where I am going'?"

Jesus continued, "You are from below; I am from above. You belong to this world; I do not. That is why I said that you will die in your sins; for unless you believe that I AM who I claim to be, you will die in your sins."

Sin happens. At the core of your being, you are sinful. Ever since Adam and Eve disobeyed God way back in the beginning, sin has been part of the story of the whole human race. Now sin comes naturally to all of us, and it controls the way we act and think. That's why Jesus said that people are slaves to sin.

S

No matter how hard you try or how good your intentions are, it is impossible to make yourself perfect and completely stop sinning. The great news is that God will forgive you. Ask Jesus to be your Savior, tell him that you're sorry for your sins, and ask him to help you stop sinning. There is only one sin that God says cannot be forgiven. That is permanently rejecting the Holy Spirit and denying his power. Don't go there.

Are you confused about what things are sin? Pretty much everyone believes murder and stealing are sins. But are there more common sins—things you might be tempted to do on a daily basis? Basically anything that goes against God's commands to love him, love other people, and obey him is sin. That includes anything self-centered like being greedy, cheating, lying, treating people unkindly, and being proud. It includes things that hurt other people and make them feel unimportant and unloved. Anything that disobeys God's commands in the Bible is sin. Jesus said that the two most important commandments are to love God and to love your neighbor. Can you do that all the time? Probably not, but you can ask God to help you be stronger so you can obey him more and more!

Soul

Every person has a soul. It is an inner part of you . . . not like your liver or pancreas, but a part that won't show up in any X-ray. The soul is your thoughts and emotions, the center of your character and personality. It's the part of you that lives on into eternity after your physical body dies. In other words, your soul is the real you!

S

Soul

Protected Soul
Matthew 10:26-28

"Don't be afraid of those who threaten you. For the time is coming when every-thing that is covered will be revealed, and all that is secret will be made known to all. What I tell you now in the darkness, shout abroad when daybreak comes. What I whisper in your ear, shout from the housetops for all to hear!

"Don't be afraid of those who want to kill your body; they cannot touch your soul. Fear only God, who can destroy both soul and body in hell."

Rested Soul
Matthew 11:28-30

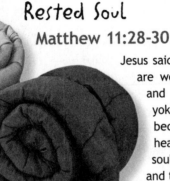

Jesus said, "Come to me, all of you who are weary and carry heavy burdens, and I will give you rest. Take my yoke upon you. Let me teach you, because I am humble and gentle at heart, and you will find rest for your souls. For my yoke is easy to bear, and the burden I give you is light."

Lost Soul
Matthew 16:24-28

Jesus said to his disciples, "If any of you wants to be my follower, you must turn from your selfish ways, take up your cross, and follow me. If you try to hang on to your life, you will lose it. But if you give up your life for my sake, you will save it. And what do you benefit if you gain the whole world but lose your own soul? Is anything worth more than your soul? For the Son of Man will come with his angels in the glory of his Father

S

and will judge all people according to their deeds. And I tell you the truth, some standing here right now will not die before they see the Son of Man coming in his Kingdom."

Dedicated Soul
Matthew 22:37-40

Jesus replied, "'You must love the LORD your God with all your heart, all your soul, and all your mind.' This is the first and greatest commandment. A second is equally important: 'Love your neighbor as yourself.' The entire law and all the demands of the prophets are based on these two commandments."

> *The word of God is alive and powerful. It is sharper than the sharpest two-edged sword, cutting between soul and spirit, between joint and marrow. It exposes our innermost thoughts and desires.*
> *—Hebrews 4:12*

You may be able to fool the people around you into thinking you are a certain kind of person—someone who is kind and caring toward others, someone who loves and honors God, someone who is honest and fair. But you can't fool God, because he sees your soul. He sees the real you. Your soul can get so covered over with the dirt of sin that it blocks out the person God wants you to be. But there's hope, because God offers to protect your soul from those who try to hurt it. It's up to you to give your soul to him—the one who made it in the first place. God also offers rest to the soul. He knows that when life gets crazy busy or really heavy with disappointment, fear, danger, or temptation, your soul gets tired. You can find rest for your soul when you trust him to take care of you. Jesus will never give you a burden that he can't help you handle.

> *My child, don't lose sight of common sense and discernment. Hang on to them, for they will refresh your soul. They are like jewels on a necklace.*
> *—Proverbs 3:21-22*

S

Strength

What does Jesus mean when he says that you can gain the whole world but lose your soul? Think about this: What if you earned a bazillion dollars and became the most famous person in the world? Imagine that you had all the stuff in the world you could possibly want. Would you be the happiest person in the world? Maybe yes, and maybe no. Most likely you wouldn't even be really happy with all your riches. That seems to be true for a lot of people who put their focus on getting more and more stuff instead of on God or what he wants for them. Even if you were happy for a while, that temporary happiness would come to a screeching halt when your life on this earth ends. You see, all the riches and fame in the world are nothing if you haven't put your trust in Jesus. So if you don't give your life to him, you will lose your soul, and the real you will go to hell, not heaven, when you die.

God wants all your love—he will not take second place to anything or anyone else. He won't share the spot of being number one in your life. So if you're going to love God, give it everything you've got. Love him completely and totally with all your heart, soul, and mind. In other words, love him with the real you!

Strength

When you think of strength, do you get an image in your mind of really muscular people, such as weight lifters or other athletes? These people train hard so their muscles are as strong as possible. Physical power is one type of strength. But what about other kinds of strength? Spiritual? Emotional? Mental?

He Will Come in Strength
Matthew 24:30-31

"At last, the sign that the Son of Man is coming will appear in the heavens, and there will be deep mourning among all the peoples of the earth. And they will see the Son of Man coming on the clouds of heaven with power and great glory. And he will send out his angels with the mighty blast of a trumpet, and they will gather his chosen ones from all over the world—from the farthest ends of the earth and heaven."

With All Your Strength
Mark 12:28-31

One of the teachers of religious law was standing there listening to the debate. He realized that Jesus had answered well, so he asked, "Of all the commandments, which is the most important?"

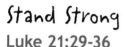

Jesus replied, "The most important commandment is this: 'Listen, O Israel! The LORD our God is the one and only LORD. And you must love the LORD your God with all your heart, all your soul, all your mind, and all your strength.' The second is equally important: 'Love your neighbor as yourself.' No other commandment is greater than these."

Stand Strong
Luke 21:29-36

[Jesus] gave them this illustration: "Notice the fig tree, or any other tree. When the leaves come out, you know without being told that summer is near. In the same way, when you see all these things taking place, you can know that the Kingdom of God is near. I tell you the truth, this generation will not pass from the scene until all these things have taken place. Heaven and earth will disappear, but my words will never disappear.

S

Strength

"Watch out! Don't let your hearts be dulled by carousing and drunkenness, and by the worries of this life. Don't let that day catch you unaware, like a trap. For that day will come upon everyone living on the earth. Keep alert at all times. And pray that you might be strong enough to escape these coming horrors and stand before the Son of Man."

A Time to Take Action
John 2:13-16

It was nearly time for the Jewish Passover celebration, so Jesus went to Jerusalem. In the Temple area he saw merchants selling cattle, sheep, and doves for sacrifices; he also saw dealers at tables exchanging foreign money. Jesus made a whip from some ropes and chased them all out of the Temple. He drove out the sheep and cattle, scattered the money changers' coins over the floor, and turned over their tables. Then, going over to the people who sold doves, he told them, "Get these things out of here. Stop turning my Father's house into a marketplace!"

> *The LORD is my strength and my song; he has given me victory.*
> —*Exodus 15:2*

Here is an amazing fact: God is stronger than any other power in the world! Seriously, think about that for a minute. God's strength raised Jesus back to life after he was crucified. His strength will bring Jesus back to earth one day to gather all his followers and take them to heaven. Jesus showed incredible strength when he was on earth. He took a stand for what was right, even when it was unpopular. For example, when he saw people in the Temple who were more concerned about making money than

S

about worshiping God, he cleared out that Temple in a flash. He knew the religious leaders wouldn't like what he did, but he had the inner strength to do it anyway. It wasn't just his physical strength people saw that day; his strength of character was obvious too.

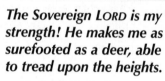

Something that's really amazing but sort of hard to understand is that God's power is available to his followers too. It is his strength inside your heart that helps you obey him and stand strong even when other people make fun of you or give you a hard time for being a Christian. Jesus said your strength should be focused on loving God with everything you've got. God never ever takes second place to anything else, so put all your energy into loving him. He is the source of true strength!

> *The Sovereign LORD is my strength! He makes me as surefooted as a deer, able to tread upon the heights.*
> *—Habakkuk 3:19*

Teachers

Has there been at least one teacher so far in your life who has been an encouragement to you—a teacher who challenged you and made learning fun and exciting? Being a teacher is a big responsibility. Schoolteachers have the challenge of teaching students about academic subjects. Spiritual teachers have the even bigger responsibility of teaching people about God.

T

Teachers

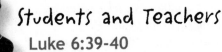

Students and Teachers
Luke 6:39-40

Jesus gave the following illustration: "Can one blind person lead another? Won't they both fall into a ditch? Students are not greater than their teacher. But the student who is fully trained will become like the teacher."

Teachers as Servants
John 13:12-20

After washing their feet, [Jesus] put on his robe again and sat down and asked, "Do you understand what I was doing? You call me 'Teacher' and 'Lord,' and you are right, because that's what I am. And since I, your Lord and Teacher, have washed your feet, you ought to wash each other's feet. I have given you an example to follow. Do as I have done to you. I tell you the truth, slaves are not greater than their master. Nor is the messenger more important than the one who sends the message. Now that you know these things, God will bless you for doing them.

"I am not saying these things to all of you; I know the ones I have chosen. But this fulfills the Scripture that says, 'The one who eats my food has turned against me.' I tell you this beforehand, so that when it happens you will believe that I AM the Messiah. I tell you the truth, anyone who welcomes my messenger is welcoming me, and anyone who welcomes me is welcoming the Father who sent me."

The Responsibility of Teachers
Matthew 5:19-20

"If you ignore the least commandment and teach others to do the same, you will be called the least in the Kingdom of Heaven. But anyone who obeys God's

T

160

laws and teaches them will be called great in the Kingdom of Heaven.

"But I warn you—unless your righteousness is better than the righteousness of the teachers of religious law and the Pharisees, you will never enter the Kingdom of Heaven!"

The Holy Spirit Teaches
John 14:25-26

"I am telling you these things now while I am still with you. But when the Father sends the Advocate as my representative—that is, the Holy Spirit—he will teach you everything and will remind you of everything I have told you."

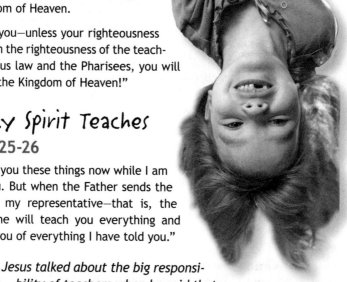

Jesus talked about the big responsibility of teachers when he said that someone who leads his or her students away from God instead of closer to him will have to answer to God himself for that. Yikes. Teachers need to always be careful about what they are saying and also about how they are living their lives. Students who admire a teacher will often make an effort to become like that teacher in the way they believe and the way they live. That's the goal, of course, with the greatest teacher—Jesus. You can learn from him by studying his words, seeing how he lived when he was on earth, and becoming more and more like him. The Holy Spirit helps with that because he lives in you and helps you understand Jesus' words. He also reminds you of them as you try to live for Jesus.

One of the biggest lessons Jesus taught his followers is that the

All Scripture is inspired by God and is useful to teach us what is true and to make us realize what is wrong in our lives. It corrects us when we are wrong and teaches us to do what is right.

—2 Timothy 3:16

T

teacher should be a servant. Think about that for a minute—teachers have great responsibility, and yet they are called to serve their students. Jesus showed that kind of humility by washing the feet of his disciples. He did the work of a servant because he truly cared about his followers. He doesn't want us to think so highly of ourselves that we want to be served

> *Fear of the LORD teaches wisdom; humility precedes honor.*
> *—Proverbs 15:33*

instead of serving. His mind-set is different from the rest of the world's. Many people are too concerned with wanting to be important and having other people respect them. Jesus taught an upside-down version of leading and teaching . . . and that's what serving others is all about.

Truth

Do you promise to tell "the truth, the whole truth, and nothing but the truth"? That's what you'd promise as a witness in a courtroom, but what about in your day-to-day life? Are there times when it's okay to stretch the truth a little? Are some lies worse than others? And most important of all, what does Jesus have to say about the truth?

God's Truth
John 3:16-21

"God loved the world so much that he gave his one and only Son, so that everyone who believes in him will not perish but have eternal life. God sent his Son into the world not to judge the world, but to save the world through him.

T

"There is no judgment against anyone who believes in him. But anyone who does not believe in him has already been judged for not believing in God's one and only Son. And the judgment is based on this fact: God's light came into the world, but people loved the darkness more than the light, for their actions were evil. All who do evil hate the light and refuse to go near it for fear their sins will be exposed. But those who do what is right come to the light so others can see that they are doing what God wants."

The Truth about Jesus
John 5:31-38

"If I were to testify on my own behalf, my testimony would not be valid. But someone else is also testifying about me, and I assure you that everything he says about me is true. In fact, you sent investigators to listen to John the Baptist, and his testimony about me was true. Of course, I have no need of human witnesses, but I say these things so you might be saved. John was like a burning and shining lamp, and you were excited for a while about his message. But I have a greater witness than John—my teachings and my miracles. The Father gave me these works to accomplish, and they prove that he sent me. And the Father who sent me has testified about me himself. You have never heard his voice or seen him face to face, and you do not have his message in your hearts, because you do not believe me—the one he sent to you."

> *Lead me by your truth and teach me,*
> *for you are the God who saves me.*
> *All day long I put my hope in you.*
> *—Psalm 25:5*

Know the Truth
John 8:31-32

Jesus said to the people who believed in him, "You are truly my disciples if you remain faithful to my teachings. And you will know the truth, and the truth will set you free."

Satan Has No Truth
John 8:44-47

"The devil . . . was a murderer from the beginning. He has always hated the truth, because there is no truth in him. When he lies, it is consistent with his character; for he is a liar and the father of lies. So when I tell the truth, you just naturally don't believe me! Which of you can truthfully accuse me of sin? And since I am telling you the truth, why don't you believe me? Anyone who belongs to God listens gladly to the words of God. But you don't listen because you don't belong to God."

Being truthful is always important, whether it's about something big or small. When you lie to your parents or friends and they discover you didn't tell the truth, your reputation is damaged and they will be less likely to trust you in the future. Jesus noted that truth is important—and the most important truth of all is about God's plan for humanity. Knowing God's truth and obeying it will help you to be truthful in all of your life. Jesus wanted people to understand the truth because accepting that truth will set you free from the sin that controls you. That's why Jesus said, "The truth will set you free." There is no other way to gain that freedom. Jesus also pointed out that Satan

Jesus Christ was revealed as God's Son by his baptism in water and by shedding his blood on the cross—not by water only, but by water and blood. And the Spirit, who is truth, confirms it with his testimony.

—1 John 5:6

doesn't know the truth, and therefore everything he says and teaches is a lie. It's easy to fall under Satan's power because he is sneaky and he makes his lies sound so convincing. The presence of the Holy Spirit in your heart will help you see the difference between the real truth and the lies that Satan throws at you. Know the truth—it's the only way to freedom!

The Work of God

How do you feel about having work to do—whether it's homework, yard work, schoolwork, or chores around the house? Maybe these things aren't your number one favorite activity. But did you know that you have a part in God's work on the earth? This isn't like cleaning your room or cutting the grass. This is an exciting adventure— being part of God's plan to share his love and salvation with all people on earth. Seriously . . . don't you want to sign up for that?

Jesus' Work
John 4:34-38

Jesus explained: "My nourishment comes from doing the will of God, who sent me, and from finishing his work. You know the saying, 'Four months between planting and harvest.' But I say, wake up and look around. The fields are already ripe for harvest. The harvesters are paid good wages, and the fruit they

W

The Work of God

harvest is people brought to eternal life. What joy awaits both the planter and the harvester alike! You know the saying, 'One plants and another harvests.' And it's true. I sent you to harvest where you didn't plant; others had already done the work, and now you will get to gather the harvest."

Jesus Obeys
John 5:19-23

Jesus explained, "I tell you the truth, the Son can do nothing by himself. He does only what he sees the Father doing. Whatever the Father does, the Son also does. For the Father loves the Son and shows him everything he is doing. In fact, the Father will show him how to do even greater works than healing this man. Then you will truly be astonished. For just as the Father gives life to those he raises from the dead, so the Son gives life to anyone he wants. In addition, the Father judges no one. Instead, he has given the Son absolute authority to judge, so that everyone will honor the Son, just as they honor the Father. Anyone who does not honor the Son is certainly not honoring the Father who sent him."

Jesus Heals
John 9:3-7

"It was not because of his sins or his parents' sins," Jesus answered. "This happened so the power of God could be seen in him. We must quickly carry out the tasks assigned us by the one who sent us. The night is coming, and then no one can work. But while I am here in the world, I am the light of the world."

> *Praise him for his mighty works; praise his unequaled greatness!*
>
> *—Psalm 150:2*

Then he spit on the ground, made mud with the saliva, and spread the mud over the blind man's eyes.

He told him, "Go wash yourself in the pool of Siloam" (Siloam means "sent"). So the man went and washed and came back seeing!

God never gets distracted from his plan. His plan from the beginning of time has been to have a personal relationship with people, so his work always centers on that. Jesus knew that his purpose on earth was to do God's work, and he did that every day with all his energy. He found fulfillment in doing that. Jesus wants the message of God's love and care to be spread throughout the earth, and he set a good example for that himself. He knows that we can't do his work on our own—that's why he said that God's strength is so important. God's strength will help you do the work he has for you in sharing his message. Don't worry if you don't know how to do something or are unsure what to say—ask God to help you.

Sometimes the work of God is seen in amazing ways. When Jesus healed the sick or raised dead people back to life, God's power was clearly seen. That was one of the ways God's work was spread throughout the world. What does that mean in your life? The things you do and say can show other people about who God is and how much he loves them. The longer you walk with God, the more ways he will show you to be part of his work. Remember, though, that you don't have to do his work in your own strength (in fact, you can't). God is the one who will give you the ability to do his work, and he will provide the help you need.

> *I am certain that God, who began the good work within you, will continue his work until it is finally finished on the day when Christ Jesus returns.*
>
> *—Philippians 1:6*

W

The World

When you think about God at work, do you tend to think in terms of your church, your hometown, or maybe your country? It's true that God is involved in those places . . . but he's also at work throughout the world! From rural farms to the inner city, from tiny islands to the tallest mountain, from the United States to Haiti to India—God made the whole world, and he's present everywhere!

The Father's Kingdom
Matthew 13:37-43

Jesus replied, "The Son of Man is the farmer who plants the good seed. The field is the world, and the good seed represents the people of the Kingdom. The weeds are the people who belong to the evil one. The enemy who planted the weeds among

W

the wheat is the devil. The harvest is the end of the world, and the harvesters are the angels.

"Just as the weeds are sorted out and burned in the fire, so it will be at the end of the world. The Son of Man will send his angels, and they will remove from his Kingdom everything that causes sin and all who do evil. And the angels will throw them into the fiery furnace, where there will be weeping and gnashing of teeth. Then the righteous will shine like the sun in their Father's Kingdom. Anyone with ears to hear should listen and understand!"

Preach to the World
Mark 16:15-18

[Jesus] told them, "Go into all the world and preach the Good News to everyone. Anyone who believes and is baptized will be saved. But anyone who refuses to believe will be condemned. These miraculous signs will accompany those who believe: They will cast out demons in my name, and they will speak in new languages.

They will be able to handle snakes with safety, and if they drink anything poisonous, it won't hurt them. They will be able to place their hands on the sick, and they will be healed."

A Light in the World
John 12:44-50

Jesus shouted to the crowds, "If you trust me, you are trusting not only me, but also God who sent me. For when you see me, you are seeing the one who sent me. I have come as a light to shine in this dark world, so that all who put their trust in me will no longer remain in the dark. I will not judge those who hear me but don't obey me, for I have come to save the world and not to judge it. But all who reject me and my message will be judged

> *You are the light of the world—like a city on a hilltop that cannot be hidden.*
>
> *—Matthew 5:14*

W

The World

on the day of judgment by the truth I have spoken. I don't speak on my own authority. The Father who sent me has commanded me what to say and how to say it. And I know his commands lead to eternal life; so I say whatever the Father tells me to say."

God's world is bigger than we realize . . . and so are his plans! God's desire is that all people of the world will have an opportunity to hear about him before Jesus comes back to take his family to heaven. Ever since the early days of Christianity, there have been missionaries who left home and went around the world to help others and share God's love.

> *Do everything without complaining and arguing, so that no one can criticize you. Live clean, innocent lives as children of God, shining like bright lights in a world full of crooked and perverse people.*
> —*Philippians 2:14-15*

Jesus was a light in a dark world, and he said that his children are to be lights too. What does a light do? It shows what is hidden in the darkness. Think about the world as a big, dark room—so dark that you can't see your own hand in front of your face. Even if your light is tiny, it will be seen in that dark room, right? The world is bigger than your hometown, and there are people around the world who seriously need to know about God's love. Jesus gave instructions to get out of your comfort zone and share his love in all places that are in darkness.

W

Worry

Okay, let's be honest: most of the time what's behind worry is, how does this situation affect me? Worry happens because we're concerned about our own future or image or reputation or comfort . . . you get the idea. Some of the stuff we worry about never even happens and isn't that huge of a deal in the big picture. But other things are really scary and feel like they're going to swallow us whole. As followers of Jesus, how are we supposed to handle these things?

Worry Does No Good
Luke 12:22-34

Turning to his disciples, Jesus said, "That is why I tell you not to worry about everyday life—whether you have enough food to eat or enough clothes to wear. For life is more than food, and your body more than clothing. Look at the ravens. They don't plant or harvest or store food in barns, for God feeds them. And you are far more valuable to him than any birds! Can all your worries add a single moment to your life? And if worry can't accomplish a little thing like that, what's the use of worrying over bigger things?

"Look at the lilies and how they grow. They don't work or make their clothing, yet Solomon in all his glory was not dressed as beautifully as they are. And if God cares so wonderfully for flowers that are here today and thrown into the fire tomorrow, he will certainly care for you. Why do you have so little faith?

"And don't be concerned about what to eat and what to drink. Don't worry about such things. These things dominate the thoughts of unbelievers all over the world, but your Father already knows your needs. Seek the Kingdom of God above all else, and he will give you everything you need.

> *Worry weighs a person down; an encouraging word cheers a person up.*
> —*Proverbs 12:25*

W

171

"So don't be afraid, little flock. For it gives your Father great happiness to give you the Kingdom.

"Sell your possessions and give to those in need. This will store up treasure for you in heaven! And the purses of heaven never get old or develop holes. Your treasure will be safe; no thief can steal it and no moth can destroy it. Wherever your treasure is, there the desires of your heart will also be."

Worry Affects Faith
Matthew 13:1-9, 18-23

Later that same day Jesus left the house and sat beside the lake. A large crowd soon gathered around him, so he got into a boat. Then he sat there and taught as the people stood on the shore. He told many stories in the form of parables, such as this one:

"Listen! A farmer went out to plant some seeds. As he scattered them across his field, some seeds fell on a footpath, and the birds came and ate them. Other seeds fell on shallow soil with underlying rock. The seeds sprouted quickly because the soil was shallow. But the plants soon wilted under the hot sun, and since they didn't have deep roots, they died. Other seeds fell among thorns that grew up and choked out the tender plants. Still other seeds fell on fertile soil, and they produced a crop that was thirty, sixty, and even a hundred times as much as had been planted! Anyone with ears to hear should listen and understand." . . .

> *You will keep in perfect peace all who trust in you, all whose thoughts are fixed on you!*
> —*Isaiah 26:3*

"Now listen to the explanation of the parable about the farmer planting seeds: The seed that fell on the footpath represents those who hear the message about the Kingdom and don't understand it. Then the evil one comes and snatches away the seed that was planted in their hearts. The seed on the rocky soil represents those who hear the message

W

and immediately receive it with joy. But since they don't have deep roots, they don't last long. They fall away as soon as they have problems or are persecuted for believing God's word. The seed that fell among the thorns represents those who hear God's word, but all too quickly the message is crowded out by the worries of this life and the lure of wealth, so no fruit is produced. The seed that fell on good soil represents those who truly hear and understand God's word and produce a harvest of thirty, sixty, or even a hundred times as much as had been planted!"

Don't Worry . . . Trust
Luke 8:40-56

On the other side of the lake the crowds welcomed Jesus, because they had been waiting for him. Then a man named Jairus, a leader of the local synagogue, came and fell at Jesus' feet, pleading with him to come home with him. His only daughter, who was about twelve years old, was dying.

As Jesus went with him, he was surrounded by the crowds. A woman in the crowd had suffered for twelve years with constant bleeding, and she could find no cure. Coming up behind Jesus, she touched the fringe of his robe. Immediately, the bleeding stopped.

"Who touched me?" Jesus asked.

Everyone denied it, and Peter said, "Master, this whole crowd is pressing up against you."

But Jesus said, "Someone deliberately touched me, for I felt healing power go out from me." When the woman realized that she could not stay hidden, she began to tremble and fell to her knees in front of him. The whole crowd heard her explain why she had touched him and that she had been immediately healed. "Daughter," he said to her, "your faith has made you well. Go in peace."

While he was still speaking to her, a messenger arrived from the home of Jairus, the leader of the synagogue. He told him, "Your daughter is dead. There's no use troubling the Teacher now."

But when Jesus heard what had happened, he said to Jairus, "Don't be afraid. Just have faith, and she will be healed."

W

Worship

When they arrived at the house, Jesus wouldn't let anyone go in with him except Peter, John, James, and the little girl's father and mother. The house was filled with people weeping and wailing, but he said, "Stop the weeping! She isn't dead; she's only asleep."

But the crowd laughed at him because they all knew she had died. Then Jesus took her by the hand and said in a loud voice, "My child, get up!" And at that moment her life returned, and she immediately stood up! Then Jesus told them to give her something to eat. Her parents were overwhelmed, but Jesus insisted that they not tell anyone what had happened.

It's normal to worry once in a while. But here's the thing—when you realize that your thoughts are being taken over by worry, it's time to take action. That's a sure sign you need to spend a few minutes remembering that God is in control of everything and that he loves you more than you can imagine. Ask him to grow your faith and trust in him. Stop and remember how he has taken care of you and your loved ones in the past. Learning to trust God enough to stop worrying is a journey, so take it a step at a time . . . and soon enough you'll find that your default mode will be trust, not worry.

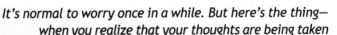

Worship

Maybe you think worship only happens on Sunday morning. After all, it's really not something you hear about much outside of a church setting. But actually everyone worships something, even

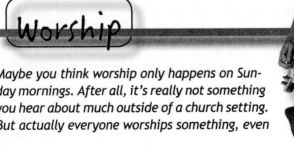

W

if it's not God. They might not call it that, but a lot of people worship athletes, musicians, or movie stars. Some people worship money or a relationship or even themselves. If something consumes your attention and your heart, there is surely an element of worship in your attitude toward it!

Be Careful Who You Worship!
Matthew 4:8-10

The devil took [Jesus] to the peak of a very high mountain and showed him all the kingdoms of the world and their glory. "I will give it all to you," he said, "if you will kneel down and worship me."

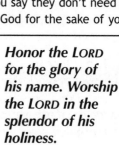

"Get out of here, Satan," Jesus told him. "For the Scriptures say, 'You must worship the LORD your God and serve only him.'"

Is Your Heart in It?
Matthew 15:3-9

Jesus replied, "And why do you, by your traditions, violate the direct commandments of God? For instance, God says, 'Honor your father and mother,' and 'Anyone who speaks disrespectfully of father or mother must be put to death.' But you say it is all right for people to say to their parents, 'Sorry, I can't help you. For I have vowed to give to God what I would have given to you.' In this way, you say they don't need to honor their parents. And so you cancel the word of God for the sake of your own tradition. You hypocrites! Isaiah was right when he prophesied about you, for he wrote,

'These people honor me with their lips,
but their hearts are far from me.
Their worship is a farce,
for they teach man-made ideas as commands
from God.'"

> *Honor the LORD for the glory of his name. Worship the LORD in the splendor of his holiness.*
>
> *—Psalm 29:2*

W

In Spirit and Truth
John 4:21-24

Jesus replied, "Believe me, dear woman, the time is coming when it will no longer matter whether you worship the Father on this mountain or in Jerusalem. You Samaritans know very little about the one you worship, while we Jews know all about him, for salvation comes through the Jews. But the time is coming—indeed it's here now—when true worshipers will worship the Father in spirit and in truth. The Father is looking for those who will worship him that way. For God is Spirit, so those who worship him must worship in spirit and in truth."

Okay, so everyone worships something. Of course, the best one to worship is God. In fact, he's really the only one worthy of worship. There is a community element to worship, but it's also a personal, individual thing. How you worship God—what brings you to the point of worship—is different for pretty much each person.

Jesus gave warnings about a couple of things in relation to worship. He warned Satan that Scripture says only God should be worshiped. Satan is always trying to pull people away from worshiping God. Dangerous stuff, huh? Jesus also pointed out that it's only worship when your heart is in it. Just because you grew up going to church every Sunday and know the "right" things to do and say in youth group does not automatically mean that you are truly worshiping God. Don't put on a show of worshiping God if your heart isn't in it. You may fool other people, but you will never fool God. He knows what is really going on in your heart.

Worship is described as a response to who God is. So when you actually understand in your heart who God is, how much he loves you, and what his plan is for the future, your response to that becomes your worship. Worship is personal, so you can certainly do it alone—you don't have to wait until Sunday morning rolls around. But worshiping with other people is important too, because it's an encouragement to others. It binds you together with other believers as brothers and sisters in God's family.

> *Come, let us worship and bow down. Let us kneel before the LORD our maker, for he is our God.*
>
> *—Psalm 95:6-7*

Worthiness

Everyone wants to matter . . . to someone. You want to believe that you are important enough that your presence in this world is noticed by another person. Well, regardless of what else is happening in your world, you do matter to God. And what makes you worthy of being noticed in God's eyes? It's not your looks or your brains or your money. . . . It's your heart.

Love God Most
Matthew 10:37-38

"If you love your father or mother more than you love me, you are not worthy of being mine; or if you love your son or daughter more than me, you are not worthy of being mine. If you refuse to take up your cross and follow me, you are not worthy of being mine."

W

Worthiness

Be a Worthy Servant
Luke 12:42-48

The Lord replied, "A faithful, sensible servant is one to whom the master can give the responsibility of managing his other household servants and feeding them. If the master returns and finds that the servant has done a good job, there will be a reward. I tell you the truth, the master will put that servant in charge of all he owns. But what if the servant thinks, 'My master won't be back for a while,' and he begins beating the other servants, partying, and getting drunk? The master will return unannounced and unexpected, and he will cut the servant in pieces and banish him with the unfaithful.

Above all, you must live as citizens of heaven, conducting yourselves in a manner worthy of the Good News about Christ. Then, whether I come and see you again or only hear about you, I will know that you are standing together with one spirit and one purpose, fighting together for the faith, which is the Good News.

—Philippians 1:27

"And a servant who knows what the master wants, but isn't prepared and doesn't carry out those instructions, will be severely punished. But someone who does not know, and then does something wrong, will be punished only lightly. When someone has been given much, much will be required in return; and when someone has been entrusted with much, even more will be required."

The Younger Son
Luke 15:11-24

To illustrate the point further, Jesus told them this story: "A man had two sons. The younger son told his father, 'I want my share of your estate now before you die.' So his father agreed to divide his wealth between his sons.

"A few days later this younger son packed all his belongings and moved to a distant land, and there he wasted all his money in wild living. About the time

W

178

his money ran out, a great famine swept over the land, and he began to starve. He persuaded a local farmer to hire him, and the man sent him into his fields to feed the pigs. The young man became so hungry that even the pods he was feeding the pigs looked good to him. But no one gave him anything.

"When he finally came to his senses, he said to himself, 'At home even the hired servants have food enough to spare, and here I am dying of hunger! I will go home to my father and say, "Father, I have sinned against both heaven and you, and I am no longer worthy of being called your son. Please take me on as a hired servant."'"

"So he returned home to his father. And while he was still a long way off, his father saw him coming. Filled with love and compassion, he ran to his son, embraced him, and kissed him. His son said to him, 'Father, I have sinned against both heaven and you, and I am no longer worthy of being called your son.'

"But his father said to the servants, 'Quick! Bring the finest robe in the house and put it on him. Get a ring for his finger and sandals for his feet. And kill the calf we have been fattening. We must celebrate with a feast, for this son of mine was dead and has now returned to life. He was lost, but now he is found.' So the party began."

If you are searching for a sense of worth, you don't have to go out and do something amazing or make a load of money or get a bunch of people to like you. You are worthy because of who God made you to be. God looks at the heart, and if your heart loves God most of all—even more than your own friends and family—you have found worthiness in God's family. Now that doesn't mean you ignore or disrespect the people in your life.

W

Worthiness

> We keep on praying for you, asking our God to enable you to live a life worthy of his call. May he give you the power to accomplish all the good things your faith prompts you to do.
>
> —2 Thessalonians 1:11

Nope, it just means that you love God so much you are willing to do whatever he asks, even if it means making big sacrifices. God wants to always be most important to you. In God's eyes, worthiness is also seen in your honesty and hard work. Jesus said it's important that you can be trusted with the work God gives you to do. People who work hard and show they are honest will be given more privileges . . . and more responsibilities. Sounds like work . . . but it's an honor and an adventure to be considered worthy of doing God's work.

And even if you mess up and don't obey God, when you come back to him he will forgive you and restore your relationship with him. That's because . . . you matter to him! He celebrates when his children who have wandered away come back, just as the father of the lost son celebrated when that son returned. You can't even imagine how much you matter to God. In his eyes, you are worthy of his love and care!

W

Ready for more?
The NLT Kids Bible
is the perfect Bible
for kids like you!

It makes reading the Bible easy.

This new Bible has several special features
that break down ideas—and help you
understand the Bible better!

The NLT Kids Bible is just the right fit for you.

www.tyndale.com/kids

CP0208